The Lamb and His Enemies

The Lamb
and
His Enemies

*Understanding the
Book of Revelation*

RUBEL SHELLY

21st Century Christian
2809 Granny White Pike
Nashville, Tennessee
37204

Table of Contents

Introduction

Introduction

No book is the work of a single individual. In the case of *The Lamb and His Enemies*, there have been many contributors. I would be most ungrateful not to begin this volume with an expression of appreciation to some of the key persons who have whetted my appetite for the book of Revelation and who have given me helpful insights relevant to its interpretation.

My first formal study of the Apocalypse was under the late *H. A. Dixon* during my undergraduate days at Freed-Hardeman College. He communicated an appreciation for all things spiritual. His attachment to and skill in teaching Revelation to young college students was phenomenal.

The second person who attempted to help me with Revelation in a formal setting was *W. B. West, Jr.* In a graduate course at Harding Graduate School of Religion, he pointed me to additional resource materials on apocalyptic literature in general and contributed his own godly discernment to my studies.

Then, of course, there are the myriad published works on Revelation which have been available to me over the years. A bibliography at the end of this volume identifies some of the works found most helpful. These are referred to in the text of this book by author's name only. Unless specific page numbers are cited in parentheses, the reference is to the appropriate section of the commentary where the verses in question are treated.

My excellent secretary, *Amy Jones*, transcribed a series of lessons I delivered on Revelation as a starting point for the writing of this volume. My dear wife, *Myra*, typed most of the final draft of the book.

Several friends and fellow-servants of the Lamb offered their services in proofreading the final manuscript. *Ann Lee, Corine Jackson, and Virgil and Oleita Bradford* spent hours of their valuable time in checking scripture references, spelling, and other details necessary for the publication of a book. I thank each of them for the donation of their valuable time to this project.

Finally, I thank the many *students of mine* – both in school and local church settings – who have taught me, pressed me to pursue some point further, and simply encouraged my interest in Revelation by their own.

To God be the glory for any help that comes to anyone in studying the Apocalypse with this book as an aid.

Rubel Shelly

Chapter One

A Book to be Understood

Revelation 1:1-3

Suggest the study of the book of Revelation, and you are likely to meet resistance. "Why in the world would anyone want to waste time with Revelation?" someone will ask. "Why, nobody can understand Revelation," another will say. I once heard of an adult Sunday School class that undertook to study through the New Testament. Beginning with Matthew, the group worked through the Gospels, Acts, Paul's epistles, and the general epistles. Then, on the threshold of one of the most exciting studies in all of sacred literature, the entire class agreed that it would be pointless to try to study Revelation and went back to Matthew again.

Revelation is the capstone book of Holy Scripture. It completes and crowns the unfolding of the message of God which began to be put into written form at the hand of Moses in the fifteenth century before the birth of Jesus.

Why, then, do so many people shy away from the book? Its heavy symbolism and strange figures of speech are foreign to our ordinary thought patterns; one has to go to the trouble of setting Revelation into its proper literary and historical context in order to read it with profit. But probably more people have been scared off the book by its abuse. Religious charlatans have used Revelation to "prove" some of the most bizarre and far-fetched schemes imaginable. As one bumps into these strange and contradictory interpretations, he is likely to turn away from Revelation with a sense of hopeless confusion–if not disgust.

God did not include this book in Holy Scripture to confuse and mystify his people. It is there *to reveal* rather than hide, *to be understood* rather than avoided. The first word of the Greek text of the book (*apokalypsis*) means "revelation, disclosure" (Arndt-Gingrich), "an uncovering" (Thayer). As Thayer observes of the word, its use in the New Testament (cf. Luke 2:32; Rom. 16:25; Gal. 1:12; 2 Thess. 1:7, *et al.*) identifies "a disclosure of truth, instruction concerning divine things before unknown." Thus one should come to Revelation expecting to learn, expecting to gain insights, expecting to have questions answered rather than created.

Indeed, the first of the seven beatitudes of the Apocalypse (cf. 1:3; 14:13; 16:15; 19:9; 20:6; 22:7,14) pronounces a blessing on those who will hear and heed the message of the book. "Blessed is he that readeth, and they that hear the words of the prophecy, and keep the things that are written therein: for the time is at hand" (Rev. 1:3). Then, in case anyone missed this invitation to understanding at the opening of the book, another is given near its conclusion as the sixth beatitude. "Blessed

9

is he that keepeth the words of the prophecy of this book" (Rev. 22:7b).

The Apocalypse is *a book to be understood,* and this volume is dedicated to assisting you deal with the book in a clear and helpful manner.

Keys to Understanding Revelation

Two important things must be kept in mind constantly as one works through the book of Revelation. We shall refer to these as "keys" to the proper interpretation of the book.

Historical Setting of the Apocalypse

One key to the understanding of the book is to be found in *a proper appreciation of the historical setting of the Revelation.*

The Roman Empire had long sought a means for unifying its far-flung territories and diverse peoples. Military power could conquer large groups of people without winning their love and loyalty, so the emperors were faced with the task of creating a sense of oneness among them. One of many attempts to achieve this purpose involved the use of religion.

The Pantheon was built in Rome to house all the major gods of the empire; the pragmatic rather than theological motivation for such a temple was to turn the hearts of the devout to the Imperial City. Beyond this, the emperors of Rome were routinely elevated to the status of deity upon their death; anyone worshipping a deceased emperor would be less likely to exhibit disloyalty to the empire in his behavior. This cult of the emperor was never very popular or taken very seriously in the early days of the empire.

The emperor cult came to be taken quite seriously in the closing years of the first Christian century, however, and grew powerful enough to pose a serious threat to the existence of the church of Christ. Although Nero (A.D. 54-68) had led a persecution of Christians in and around Rome during the last year of his reign, it was Domitian (A.D. 81-96) who has the dubious distinction of being the first Roman ruler to lead an empire-wide persecution of the church. Not content to wait until death for the senate to confer deity upon him, he proclaimed himself *dominus et deus* (Latin, "Lord and God") and required worship from his subjects. One's willingness to offer such worship was taken (rather naively) to signify the supplicant's loyalty to the empire Domitian headed; one's unwillingness to worship at an imperial shrine was regarded as both irreverent and treasonous.

Long before Domitian's elevation of the emperor cult, Paul had enunciated the principle which made conflict with it inevitable on the part of the church. To Christians at Corinth, he wrote: "For though there be that are called gods, whether in heaven or on earth; as there are gods many, and lords many; yet to us there is *one God, the Father,* of whom are all things, and we unto him; and *one Lord, Jesus Christ,* through whom are all things, and we through him" (1 Cor. 8:5-6; cf. Eph. 4:4-5; Acts 4:12). Although the Jewish people were exempted from the requirement of

10

emperor worship because of their long-recognized monotheism, the Christians were held liable to it. So when faithful Christians refused to acknowledge Domitian as "Lord and God" and refused to put incense on his altar, they became objects of hatred and persecution. Vicious lies began to be circulated about them, and official sanctions were applied with varying degrees of intensity by officials in different locations throughout the empire. Believers in Christ became liable to arrest, economic boycott, and even death (cf. Rev. 13:5-10).

The book of Revelation was written to Christians in this crisis situation. It was designed to *comfort* believers who were being persecuted for Christ's sake, to *exhort* the saints to bear their trials with patience and hope, and to *warn* the enemies of the church about their impending overthrow and destruction.

The human penman of the Apocalypse, the apostle John, was himself in exile on a barren island in the Aegean Sea when he received the Revelation. "I John, your brother and partaker with you in the tribulation and kingdom and patience which are in Jesus, was in the isle that is called Patmos, for the word of God and the testimony of Jesus" (Rev. 1:9). While in that lonely place and separated in his old age from the Christians for whom he bore such consuming concern, he was given a series of messages and visions about the struggle between Rome and the church which were to be communicated to the believers of the Roman province of Asia.

"The Revelation of Jesus Christ, which God gave him to show unto his servants, even the things which must shortly come to pass: and he sent and signified it by his angel unto his servant John; who bare witness of the word of God, and of the testimony of Jesus Christ, even of all things that he saw" (Rev. 1:1-2). Here, then, is the source of everything found in the final book of our English Bibles. It is "The Revelation of Jesus Christ" (i.e., a disclosure of truth by Jesus Christ) which he sent to the saints of Asia through John. Knowing the mind of deity and aware of what the future held, Jesus made much of this information available to John through a revealing angel who is referred to frequently in the book. From the Godhead to Jesus, from Jesus to the angel, from the angel to John, and from John to the persecuted saints of Asia, secrets about the outcome of this life-or-death struggle were communicated.

John's home was at Ephesus, and the Lord had him to send this letter originally to the church there and to six other centrally located congregations of the province (Rev. 1:11). Sir William Ramsay has pointed out that the seven churches of Asia (i.e., Ephesus, Smyrna, Pergamum, Thyatira, Sardis, Philadelphia, and Laodicea) were strategically located on a rather circular route from which the book's contents would have circulated to all the saints in the area. Since Christians all through the empire were sharing a similar fate, all of them would have profited from receiving it.

Irenaeus wrote in the late second century and said the Apocalypse was produced "toward the end of the reign of Domitian" (*Against Her-*

11

esies 5. 30. 3.). Eusebius, a fourth-century church historian, preserves the same tradition and adds that John returned to his home at Ephesus following the death of Domitian (*Church History* 3. 20.). This means that the book should be dated somewhere around A.D. 95.

Although some argue for an earlier date, the following facts tend to give strong support for the late date to be presupposed henceforth in this book. First, the cult of emperor worship is clearly reflected in the book. As already indicated, however, emperor worship was not a significant factor in the empire before Domitian. Second, the persecutions reflected in the book are widespread. Saints were being severely abused; Antipas (if not others, cf. Rev. 2:13; 6:9) had already been martyred, and even greater ordeals were just ahead. The persecutions under Nero in the mid-60s simply were not empire-wide or so extensive as those described here. Third, the conditions of the seven churches suggest a date near the close of the first century. For example, Paul wrote the Ephesians around A.D. 60-62, and the church was relatively healthy in terms of its spiritual condition; by the time of the letter to Ephesus in Revelation 2:1-7, it had deteriorated so badly that it was said to have left its first love. Also, R. H. Charles makes a rather strong case for the fact that the church at Smyrna did not even exist until around A.D. 60-64.

One cannot expect to understand Revelation divorced from this sort of information about the circumstances of its production. Christians were facing the grim ordeal of persecution, and this book was given them to reveal "the things which must shortly come to pass" (1:1b). The word of significance in this verse is "shortly." Of what possible value would it have been to write a letter to agonizing saints of the first century to tell them about the papacy, Mohammed, Adolf Hitler, nuclear weapons, modern Israel, and the like? Finding these things in the book makes it meaningless to the people who were its original recipients and leads to fanciful and absurd interpretations. *Revelation is a spawning ground for theological nonsense when interpreted in isolation from its historical context and purpose.*

Apocalyptic Literature

Another key to the interpretation of Revelation is *an acquaintance with a type of Hebrew literature known as apocalyptic literature.* During the period from 200 B.C. to A.D. 200, a great deal of this sort of material surfaced among the Jewish people. Patterned after the Old Testament books of Daniel and Ezekiel, along with parts of Zechariah, this style of literature was intended not to obscure a writer's message but to make it the more vivid and impressive through the use of dramatic figures.

Apocalypses tended to appear in times of extreme difficulty in order to convey an optimistic message. The *general theme* of all such writings may be summarized as follows: *God is in ultimate control of history and fully capable of bringing men and events to his desired ends.*

Many apocalypses (i.e., revelations) were in circulation by the time John received this message on Patmos. The book of Revelation is not unique in that it is apocalyptic in style; its uniqueness lies in the fact that it is an *inspired* (i.e., God-breathed, cf. 2 Tim. 3:16-17 NIV) apocalypse. But because it is the only book of this style in the New Testament, it seems stranger, more remote, more forbidding, and more difficult to most of us. All the more reason, then, to understand something of the general nature of such literature before attempting to interpret the Revelation.

Apocalyptic literature has a number of typical features, and we need to study the final book of the New Testament canon against the background of an appreciation of those features.

First, all apocalyptic books *reflect dark times in human history.* For example, the most important non-biblical apocalypse known to us is the *Book of Enoch* or *1 Enoch.* Under the rule of Antiochus Epiphanes (175-165 B.C.), the Jewish people experienced the plundering of their temple and a host of atrocities. Under these terrible conditions, *1 Enoch* was produced to hold out hope to the people of better times when "the Son of Man" would appear oneday. Second, an apocalypse *personifies good and evil in a situation of conflict.* Animals are often used to represent men and nations, and their struggles are like horror-movie fights to the death. Third, *predictions are made* about the outcome of the struggle being pictured and the fate of the wicked figures in the drama. Fourth, the message is made known through *visions.* Fifth, a *common symbolism* is employed in the apocalypses. God's people are represented by domesticated animals; the evil forces set against God are represented by wild beasts. Numbers are important: two = something strengthened, three = the divine number, four = the world men inhabit, six = imperfection or evil, seven = perfection, ten and its multiples = human completeness, twelve = organized religion. Also, colors have special meaning: white = purity, red = blood, black = death. Sixth, apocalypses are usually *untraceable as to their authorship.* Seventh, an apocalypse is *typically said to have been "sealed"* (i.e., closed and its contents hidden) for future generations to discover.

Revelation shares the first five of these common traits and differs in the last two. It certainly reflects a dark time in history; the church is under attack from Rome and all its allied forces. It personifies good and evil in conflict; the Lamb (i.e., Christ) and the dragon (i.e., Satan) are battling to the death. Predictions are made about the outcome of the struggle; the saints are assured that Christ will be victorious and that they can share his victory by faithfulness to him during their ordeal. The message is made known through visions; John sees them on Patmos and writes them down "in the Spirit" (cf. Rev. 1:10). And Revelation employs the common symbols of the apocalypses in general; divine judgments against Rome are in groups of seven, the church is represented under the imagery of twelve tribes, etc.

As to authorship, however, the book is not pseudonymous. The writer calls himself John four times in the book (Rev. 1:1,4,9; 22:8). No John other than the apostle would have been so well-known among the Christians of Asia that he would need no further identification, and the tone of authority used by the writer would have been inappropriate for anyone other than an apostle (cf. Rev. 22:18-19). No dissent from this identification of the writer of Revelation occurs in history until Dionysius of Alexandria in the third century. None of his (or later) arguments against apostolic authorship are weighty enough to move one away from the traditional view of the matter.

Finally, the book is not "sealed" but intended for immediate consumption. The angel in charge of revealing the book's contents to John ordered specifically: "Seal not up the words of the prophecy of this book; for the time is at hand" (Rev. 22:10).

Although this style of literature is not common among people of our day, it was widely known among the original recipients of the Revelation. John was a Jew by birth and was familiar with apocalyptic style. And while not every Christian in Asia would have been familiar with the details of apocalyptic literature (for they were predominantly Gentile believers), the "messengers" (Gk, *angeloi*) charged with making the book's message known within the churches certainly must have been (cf. Rev. 2:1, 8, 12, 18; 3:1, 7, 14).

The employment of this style of writing was ideal for the circumstances under which Revelation was written. The use of symbols instead of name-calling prose allowed its circulation among the churches without government suppression. Yet, among its original readers, the book's imagery would have been as clear as today's use of such figures as Uncle Sam, the Russian bear, the Democratic donkey, or the Republican elephant is to people who read the political cartoons in our newspapers.

Even if some of the symbols are not as clear to us as they would have been to the book's first readers, there is no excuse for mistaking its message. *Revelation is an assurance that God's way of truth and righteousness will triumph over all its foes.* Christians of every age – particularly those who live in situations of great opposition and stress – can read this book and take heart over the fact that God is in control of history.

Our Approach to the Book

Our method of studying Revelation will be dictated by the two "keys" to understanding just identified. Above all else, *we shall attempt to interpret the book so as to allow for a meaningful message to its first-century readers.* Insofar as it is humanly possible to do so, *we shall read the book through the eyes of a first-century Christian living in the Roman province of Asia.* Allowing for the literary style of the book, *we shall see its symbols as pointing to the struggle such a person and his contemporaries were experiencing with mighty Rome.*

This approach to the Apocalypse sees it as a *prophecy* (cf. 1:3a) about the outcome of a great struggle between the church and the empire. The

14

book shows God's presence among his persecuted people, and it assures victory to those who will keep the faith. In one sense, it could be argued that Revelation is the filling out of the promise of Christ in the Sermon on the Mount about the fate of those who are called upon to suffer for his name. "Blessed are they that have been persecuted for righteousness' sake: for theirs is the kingdom of heaven. Blessed are ye when men shall reproach you, and persecute you, and say all manner of evil against you falsely, for my sake. Rejoice, and be exceedingly glad: for great is your reward in heaven: for so persecuted they the prophets that were before you" (Matt. 5:10-12).

Remember that one can get the main point of the prophecy of Revelation without being dogmatic about every detail of its interpretation. Some of the symbols are heavy and obscure; the message is clear and plain.

Its Importance for Us

As we begin a study of Revelation, it will be worthwhile not only to get our bearings for the sake of a correct approach to interpreting the book but also to remind ourselves why it is worth the effort to spend so much mental energy on a book many people simply avoid.

This is a revelation given by Jesus Christ (Rev. 1:1). Since it comes from him, it must be of value.

Revelation is a book whose message centers on Jesus Christ. Because of our love for the Savior, any book whose central character is Jesus must be of primary interest to us. Jesus is the glorious one who appears to John in chapter one, who moves among the churches in chapters two and three, who is the object of all heaven's adoration in chapter four, and so on through the book.

This book sets forth the Christian philosophy of history. Some view history fatalistically (i.e., what will be will be), others see it as meaningless repetition (i.e., history simply repeats itself), and still others see it as being without purpose at all (i.e., non-teleological). The Christian view of history holds that God is in ultimate control of the cosmos and that his truth and righteousness will triumph over evil. This view holds that history *is* going somewhere; it is *going to Judgment.* It is heading toward a final accounting before the Almighty God at the Great White Throne (Rev. 20:11-15).

A proper understanding of Revelation helps one avoid persons and theories which abuse its contents. Very early in this chapter the point was made that false teachers love to use the Apocalypse for the sake of subverting the weak and leading souls astray. If one of them is allowed to assign arbitary meanings to the symbols of the book and to divorce it from its historical context, he can prove anything he chooses. The best way to keep Revelation from misuse is to put it to correct use. Take the time to appreciate its setting and literary style, learn its message, and appreciate its graceful use of imagery. Henceforth you will be less likely to find any attraction in the speculative and unfounded theories of men which attempt to latch onto some part of this wonderful piece of inspired literature.

Finally, Revelation is important to us because it underscores the value of trust in God. How could the saints of the late first century survive the ordeal of persecution by the most powerful empire of history? They could learn to believe in, to trust, to commit their very souls to the Lamb of the Revelation drama. Standing with him against evil, they could experience deliverance by his power; keeping faith with him rather than yielding to Domitian's command to commit idolatry, they could exhibit the sort of integrity which God's prophets, apostles, and other heroes of faith had shown before them (cf. Heb. 11:32-38); willing to die if necessary rather than deny their true Lord and God (Rev. 2:10), they could look to a glorious resurrection and the crown of eternal life. Do saints of our own time not have trials to face? Can the faith and courage inspired by Revelation not serve to aid them?

A friend of mine who was a missionary in an unstable country told me how meaningful the study of Revelation came to be for him when his life was being threatened by a terrorist group in the nation. For others the crises have been of a very different nature. Teens who are trying to follow Christ in a school where the subculture is viciously anti-Christian have come to love the Apocalypse for its theme. Persons working in careers which subject them to special temptations and pressures have found incentive to faithfulness in Revelation. Since it is true that everyone living a really godly life will suffer some sort of opposition for it (2 Tim. 3:12), it follows that there will come days when a knowledge of Revelation's message of optimism will be just what is needed for every child of God.

Conclusion

Let the heartening, Christ-centered, and faith-generating message of the book of Revelation fill your soul. Allow your imagination to be captivated and your mind to be challenged.

As you work through the text of Revelation from your own Bible and use the helps from this volume to assist your study, it is believed that you will come to understand and appreciate it as a fitting climax to the total content of Holy Scripture. It is hoped that you will never again fear or shy away from Revelation but henceforth regard it properly as *a book to be understood*.

Thinking Through Chapter One

1. Why have people tended to avoid the study of Revelation? How does this book fit into the development of the Bible's total theme?

2. Summarize the relevant historical information one needs for an intelligent study of the Apocalypse.

3. What do we know about the human penman of Revelation?

4. What date for the writing of Revelation is assumed for this study? On what grounds?

5. What is the significance of the word "shortly" in the first verse of Revelation?

6. What other books of the Bible are written in apocalyptic style?

7. What are the typical features of apocalyptic literature?

8. Which of the typical features of apocalyptic literature does Revelation share? In which does it differ?

9. Why was the apocalyptic style so appropriate for the writing of Revelation?

10. How can you justify spending the time and effort necessary to study the Revelation?

Chapter Two

Christ's Care for the Churches

Revelation 1:4-20

The sense of being isolated, alone, and unloved can destroy an individual. Serious emotional problems are frequently traceable to a lack of affection in a person's early life. Health studies have shown that single, widowed, and divorced people are far likelier to be victims of such problems as heart disease (five times the death rate) and tuberculosis (ten times the death rate) than married people the same age. One recent study reveals that even people in deep comas frequently show improved heart rates when their hands are held.

Imagine for a moment that you are living in Roman proconsular Asia at the end of the first century of this era. You are a Christian, and for that fact alone you are shunned, your business is boycotted, and your children are not welcome to associate with people their age in the city; the walls of your house are used frequently for vulgar graffiti, and you are liable to arrest. Do you think it might begin to bother you? Could you possibly begin to feel isolated, alone, and unloved? Might your nerves be jangled, your health affected, and your faith challenged? Precisely because these things were happening among the saints of Asia, *the book of Revelation begins with an assurance of Christ's concern for his people.*

Christ loves the church supremely. "Husbands, love your wives, even as Christ also loved the church, and gave himself up for it ..." (Eph. 5:25). His death for the church (cf. Acts 20:28) was only the beginning, however, for in his resurrected state he serves now as Head of the Church and works to bring his saved people home to himself. Paul put it this way: "It is Christ Jesus that died, yea rather, that was raised from the dead, who is at the right hand of God, who also maketh intercession for us. Who shall separate us from the love of Christ? shall tribulation, or anguish, or persecution, or famine, or nakedness, or peril, or sword? ... Nay, in all these things we are more than conquerors through him that loved us" (Rom. 8:34-37).

The Savior saw fit to send a special message of comfort and reassurance to the churches of Asia to the effect that they were not alone in their ordeal of suffering. In this chapter, we shall examine the significance of John's initial vision of the Christ in the Apocalypse. We will see its relevance to the needs of the people for whom the letter was written originally – and its abiding significance for us. We shall come to appreciate the fact of Christ's constant presence with and care for the local bodies of his struggling yet faithful people.

John's Greeting to His Readers

The epistolary section of the Revelation begins in a rather typical manner: "John to the seven churches that are in Asia" (1:4a). The writer identifies himself at the beginning – as opposed to our custom of signing at the end of a letter–and names the intended readers of his work.

The apostle John, now a very old man and the last living apostle, writes from his own situation of personal exile on Patmos (1:9) to the increasingly isolated saints of the mainland. [Note: We have no way of knowing whether Revelation was sent to the believers in Asia while John was still on the island or whether its delivery had to await his return to Ephesus after the death of Domitian.] Here referred to simply as the "seven churches that are in Asia," they are named individually in verse eleven. "Asia" here does not mean, of course, the continent of Asia or the area we designate Asia Minor; it refers to a Roman province situated on the west central coast of Asia Minor.

The "seven churches" are not representative of the church of all times and all places but were actual congregations of the people of God in the cities of Ephesus, Smyrna, Pergamum, Thyatira, Sardis, Philadelphia, and Laodicea. In the next two chapters of this volume, we shall look briefly at each of these cities and the churches in them. For now it is enough to wonder why these specific congregations were singled out. There were certainly more than seven churches in Asia at this time; Colossae, for example, is located just southeast of Laodicea (cf. Col. 1:2). Perhaps these seven were the central ones for communications purposes in the province, or perhaps exactly seven churches were addressed because of the special significance of the number "seven" (i.e., perfection) to the overall nature of this apocalyptic book. We cannot say precisely why these and only these seven churches are named; we can be sure, however, that the message of the book was intended for all the saints in similar circumstances with these seven congregations of believers.

The salutation is typical of New Testament writings: "Grace to you and peace." There is something arrestingly beautiful in the way this greeting is associated with all three members of the Godhead. First, this grace and peace were "from him who is and who was and who is to come." Jewish reverence for the sacred name *Yahweh* would not allow them to pronounce it and produced instead a number of paraphrases and descriptions of the Father in heaven; John's reference to him here as the one who "is and who was and who is to come" is surely rooted in the Almighty's identification of himself to Moses at Exodus 3:14 and designed to emphasize his eternality as opposed to Rome's fleeting moment in the sun. Second, the blessing of grace and peace is also "from the seven spirits that are before his throne." Against the use of seven in apocalyptic writings to signify perfection, this is surely a manner of reference to the Holy Spirit. If this is not the case, Revelation nowhere mentions the Spirit of God. Third, grace and peace are invoked "from

Jesus Christ, who is the faithful witness, the firstborn of the dead, and the ruler of the kings of the earth." In all things Jesus is the one who gives a true witness to the things of God (cf. John 3:32) and who has set the perfect example of faithfulness in that role. In that he died rather than deny the Father, Christians under stress have a perfect model to imitate. And if a child of God should be called on to die for his or her faith (cf. Rev. 2:10), let that person remember that heaven vindicated Jesus by raising him from the dead. The same power that raised him from the dead is present in all faithful believers (cf. Rom. 8:11) and will raise and glorify them. Alive forevermore, Jesus is the "firstborn of the dead" (i.e., sovereign in the kingdom of God, cf. Psa. 89:27) and "ruler of the kings of the earth" (i.e., in control of history and able to establish or destroy human rulers—including the arrogant Caesars).

At the mention of the name "Jesus," John breaks forth into a doxology concerning the salvation he has provided: "Unto him that loveth us, and loosed us from our sins by his blood; and he made us to be a kingdom, to be priests unto his God and Father; to him be the glory and the dominion for ever and ever. Amen" (1:5b-6). Glory and dominion belong to Christ – not Rome. Because of his abiding love which prompted the once-for-all sacrifice for our sins, all those who have been cleansed by his blood are constituted a kingdom. Furthermore, this present kingdom is one in which every Christian functions as a priest to do divine service continually.

Verse seven takes John's greeting to a crescendo. "Behold, he cometh with the clouds; and every eye shall see him, and they that pierced him; and all the tribes of the earth shall mourn over him. Even so, Amen." Most people read this verse as a direct reference to the second coming of Christ at the end of time. While one need not deny that the announcement here has an ultimate fulfillment in that event, the tenor of the opening lines of Revelation is against seeing this as the primary referent. John has already emphasized that he is dealing with things "at hand" (Rev. 1:3); yet the personal second coming of Christ did not occur shortly after this writing. What did occur shortly after the writing of Revelation was a coming in judgment against Rome to execute the details of the things about to be revealed in this book. Isaiah 19:1 speaks of the Lord's coming "upon a swift cloud" against Egypt, with the result that "the idols of Egypt shall tremble at his presence." It is a more reasonable interpretation of this verse to see its immediate fulfillment in Christ's coming in judgment against Rome and to view his personal second coming as a later completion of its prediction. Either event would be known by all mankind (i.e., "every eye shall see him") and cause unbelievers to "mourn" over his presence.

The greeting closes with a second affirmation (cf. 1:4b) of the eternality of Yahweh. "I am the Alpha and the Omega, saith the Lord God, who is and who was and who is to come, the Almighty" (1:8). Although peril and persecution made their world look dark, those saints who feared Domitian were called upon to recognize that God does not abdicate his place as ruler to him or any other. He is still on his throne, and the saints are not alone in their struggles.

John's Commission to Write

John informs us of the circumstances under which he came to write this book. "I John, your brother and partaker with you in the tribulation and kingdom and patience which are in Jesus, was in the isle that is called Patmos, for the word of God and the testimony of Jesus. I was in the Spirit on the Lord's day, and I heard behind me a great voice, as a trumpet saying, What thou seest, write in a book and send it to the seven churches: unto Ephesus, and unto Smyrna, and unto Pergamum, and unto Thyatira, and unto Sardis, and unto Philadelphia, and unto Laodicea" (1:9-11).

Patmos was a prison island about seventy miles southwest of Ephesus. John had been banished there because of his loyalty to Christ and in order to separate him from all the believers who looked to him for guidance and stability. But he was not alone and abandoned on Patmos. One Sunday (i.e., "the Lord's day," cf. Charles, pp. 22-23) during his time there, he came to be "in the Spirit." Surely with his heart already filled with thoughts of God, in a spirit of worship, and conscious of his brethren worshipping back on the mainland, John was taken hold of by the Holy Spirit for the special purpose of speaking to and through him. For him to have been "in the Spirit" for the sake of the visions which follow must have been somewhat like the state experienced by Peter on the housetop in Joppa (Acts 10:9-16). Of Peter, Luke says that "he fell into a trance" (Gk, *ekstasis*). Of the word *ekstasis*, Kittel observes that its most literal meaning is "change of place"; figuratively, then, it could be used of one's being transported in spirit or mind (cf. Rev.4:2) to places, scenes, or events which did not belong to the space-time place his body was occupying.

Under the control and direct influence of the Spirit of God, John was to be allowed to see and hear things which were not part of his actual physical surroundings. It was no mere dream or mental fantasy, for these scenes were given him by God to reveal the outcome of the church's intense struggle with Rome.

Because of his banishment to the penal colony on Patmos, John could identify himself with his readers as a "brother and partaker with you in the tribulation" they were experiencing at the moment; he understood their situation and needs, for he was sharing their problems. Yet he also reminded his readers that they shared not only difficulties but also the "kingdom and patience which are in Jesus"; if they shared tribulation, they also shared something far greater. The message is beginnning to be hinted at for them: *we are not alone in our tribulation.* For one thing, we still have each other; for another, as will be made emphatic momentarily, we have a concerned Savior moving among us and seeing to our well-being in all spiritual things.

In passing, one should not fail to take note of the notion of the *kingdom* which John holds forth in the Revelation. The kingdom of God is not something to be ushered in at the end of the events about to be chronicled; Christ made us into a kingdom by virtue of loosing us from sin by his blood (1:6), and John and his contemporary brethren were partakers rather than mere anticipators of the "kingdom ... in Jesus" (1:9). People who read Revelation as a blueprint of events to precede the coming of the kingdom are overlooking the book's own perspective on the kingdom as an existing and functioning reality.

The voice John heard speaking to him was "as of a trumpet" (i.e., commanding, signifying something important) and must have been that of Christ himself (cf. vs. 17-19). The Lord instructed John to write down the things he was seeing and to circulate the record among the seven churches of Asia. The encouragement which John would derive from knowing these things was to be shared with others who needed the same assurances.

The Glorious and Caring Christ

When John heard the strong voice behind him, he turned to see its source and received his first vision of the Christ of the Apocalypse.

"And I turned to see the voice that spake with me. And having turned I saw seven golden candlesticks; and in the midst of the candlesticks one like unto a son of man, clothed with a garment down to the foot, and girt about the breasts with a golden girdle. And his head and his hair were white as white wool, white as snow; and his eyes were as a flame of fire; and his feet like unto burnished brass, as if it had been refined in a furnace; and his voice as the voice of many waters. And he had in his right hand seven stars: and out of his mouth proceeded a sharp two-edged sword: and his countenance was as the sun shineth in his strength" (1:12-16).

His Appearance

The person John saw was "one like unto a son of man." This same expression occurs in Daniel 7:13-14, and the apocalyptic vision of that Old Testament text is surely the background for the one in this passage. The Son of Man motif was picked up from Daniel and developed at great length in apocalyptic literature among the Jews (cf. reference to *1 Enoch* in Chapter One). In Daniel 7, the prophet of God in exile in Babylon saw a vision of four great beasts arising in succession from a churning sea. A scene of judgment was then witnessed, wherein fire fell and devoured the fourth beast. It was at this point in the vision that One Like the Son of Man came before the Judge (i.e., the Ancient of Days), and received an eternal and universal kingdom.

The four beasts of this passage correspond to the four parts of the great image in Daniel 2. They represent, in order, the Babylonian, Medo-Persian, Greek, and Roman Empires. Thus the vision portrays God's judgment upon all these earthly kingdoms and upon the fourth one (i.e., Rome) in particular. The fulfillment of this prophecy occurred in connection with the ascension of Christ back to the Father following his resurrection from the dead and his subsequent work on behalf of his people.

John therefore ties the figure appearing to him with that person already known to students of Scripture as the Son of Man. He brings him on the scene as having already received his kingdom from the Father and ready now to turn to its defense against those who would destroy it. The clothing of the Son of Man (i.e., a garment down to the foot) indicates one of rank and position; the robe is tied not at the waist (i.e., as a workman's) but at the breast (i.e., "the repose of sovereignty," Roberts). The clothing here sounds a bit like that worn by the high priest in the Old Testament, and may be designed to signify Christ's role as the high priest of his people—after the order of Melchizedek.

As to his person, the Christ's head and hair are white; white is always a symbol of purity in apocalyptic writings and perhaps here of dignity and wisdom as well. His eyes are like fire, penetrating and flashing (i.e., able to penetrate the depths of human hearts). His feet are like burnished brass, strong and able to crush those who would hinder his right purposes. His voice has the majestic power of many waters. From his mouth comes a sharp two-edged sword, the Word of God (cf. Heb. 4:12), and his overall countenance is as dazzling as the sun at its zenith.

While this sort of analysis of the parts of his appearance has a certain value, too much of an attempt to form a literal picture of a man with these features results in absurdity. Caird warns us against the tendency "to unweave the rainbow" here and says correctly that John's purpose is not found in each particular element of the description but in creating the "response of overwhelming and annihilating wonder" among his readers which he felt himself in response to the initial prophetic vision of the Son of Man.

In his radiance, the Savior was standing among seven golden candlesticks (i.e., lampstands) and holding seven stars in his right hand. One should not visualize the seven-pronged lampstand of the Israelite tabernacle and temple but seven free-standing and separate lampstands among which one could walk. Not left to wonder what they represent, verse twenty informs us that "the seven candlesticks are the seven churches." Jesus walks among the churches. He knows their condition. He cares for their welfare.

Represented here as lampstands, the churches do not give out a light of their own so much as they simply hold forth the light of Christ and the gospel. This is the task of every faithful congregation of the body of Christ in every age and not merely the duty of the seven churches of Asia. When any church is fulfilling that mission to the world, Christ is present with it, watching over it, and guarding it.

Further, John saw seven stars in his right hand. Again, this is interpreted for us in verse twenty: "the seven stars are the angels of the seven churches." In chapters two and three, the seven short epistles to the churches of Asia are addressed to those churches via the "angel" of each. Although the word here (Gk, *angelos*) often refers to those heavenly, spirit beings who serve God in heaven, we probably should not think in terms of "guardian angels" of the churches but of human ministers working within the churches. *Angelos* simply means "messenger" (cf. Luke 7:24; 9:52), and here likely denotes the preacher or body of bishops which would be responsible for actually presenting the content of the Apocalypse to the people within the churches. That these messengers are "in his right hand" (1:16) suggests both the special nature of their ministry and the source of their authority for the performance of it.

In all his splendor as the resurrected and glorious Son of Man, Jesus moves among the churches. He knows their progress and their perils. He upholds and strengthens those who declare and defend his message among them. *He cares about the churches, and he is not unaware of what is happening among them.* Whether suffering at the hands of the Romans in the first century or facing trials of faith in a hostile environment today, the saints of God are not alone.

John's Reaction

"And when I saw him, I fell at his feet as one dead" (1:17a). So overpowering was this initial vision of the Lord Jesus, John was overwhelmed by its force. One is reminded of John's reaction to the transfiguration of Christ over a half-century before this event, when he, James, and Peter were awestruck by the glory of the Lord witnessed on that holy mountain (cf. Matt. 17:6).

Although genuinely frightened by so wonderful a vision of the Lord, the purpose of the appearance was not to create fear but confidence. Thus the Savior acted immediately to reassure and comfort the aged apostle.

Reassurance From the Son of Man

"And he laid his right hand upon me, saying, Fear not; I am the first and the last, and the living one; and I was dead, and behold, I am alive for evermore, and I have the keys of death and Hades" (1:17b-18).

Again, as he had done on the Mount of Transfiguration, Jesus acted to calm John by touching him and telling him not to be afraid (cf. Matt.17:7). Then, in a threefold indentification of himself, he moved to sweep away John's fear by telling him how it is that his presence guarantees victory over all that might create anxiety.

First, he speaks of his eternality; Jesus is "the first and the last, and the living one." If Rome's wickedness and apparent invulnerability frightened John and the saints, they were neither surprising nor frightening to Jesus. Rome's persecution of believers was a mere "flash in the pan" to one who knows eternity. Wicked men and tormenting powers had appeared before Rome, and others would come after it. The eternal God has survived it all, and his right purposes continue to be accomplished.

Second, he speaks of his own personal resurrection; he says, "I was dead, and behold, I am alive for evermore." This is to say: John, the worst Rome can do to any one of you is to take your mortal life (cf.

25

Matt. 10:28); that was my fate at their hands while in the flesh, but see for yourself how death merely served to usher me into glory. So will it be for any of you who must suffer unto death for my sake!

Thus, third, know that "I have the keys of death and of Hades"; the resurrection not only brought Jesus to life personally but also gave him universal and eternal authority over life and death. Death cannot destroy, and Hades cannot restrain. In that Christ has conquered death, he has conquered it for all of those who believe in him.

So do not fear. Take heart for your struggle with evil, and know that you have every reason to be courageous. Your Savior has overcome, and he has a share in his glory for every one of his own who overcomes his or her special challenge. To borrow the inspired words of Paul as our summary: "For I reckon that the sufferings of this present time are not worthy to be compared with the glory which shall be revealed to us-ward" (Rom. 8:16-18).

Conclusion

What an effect this vision must have had upon John. At first lonely, in exile, separated from his beloved brethren on the Lord's day, surely he was feeling the discouragement which all of us have tasted in some particular circumstance of spiritual peril. Then, when the Lord appeared to him, John's depression gave way to terror. Finally, touched, comforted, and made secure by the Son of Man, all else became irrelevant. John had a living and life-imparting Redeemer, and Rome's threats or acts of violence against him were nothing. Since to share in Christ's suffering is also to share in his glory, John could afford to rejoice in the midst of the tribulation Satan was bringing upon him.

Is this message for John alone? Is he the only one the Lord seeks to reassure by appearing on Patmos? Of course not. Thus Jesus commands him: "Write therefore the things which thou sawest, and the things which are, and the things which shall come to pass hereafter" (1:19). The message of this book was to go forth from Patmos to every troubled, discouraged, and anxious saint.

When a suffering saint in any generation has cause to ask "Does Jesus care when my heart is pained/ Too deeply for mirth and song;/ As the burdens press, and the cares distress,/ And the way grows weary and long?", the message of the book of Revelation rings over the centuries to say "O yes, he cares; I know he cares,/ His heart is touched with my grief;/ When the days are weary, the long nights dreary/ I know my Savior cares" (Frank E. Graeff).

Jesus cares about the churches wearing his name and about every child of God in those bodies of his people.

Thinking Through Chapter Two

1. What are some of the evidences you would cite to prove the love of Christ for the church? Why is this such an important theme of Revelation?

2. Why do you suppose exactly seven churches were singled out for attention in the Revelation?

26

3. Discuss the doxology of praise to Jesus in verses five and six.

4. Do you take verse seven to be a reference to the second coming? Why or why not?

5. What is meant by the expression "in the Spirit" when it is used of John in this book?

6. What is John's notion of the kingdom of God?

7. Describe the first vision John had of the Christ.

8. Read and analyze Daniel 7:13-14. How do these Old Testament verses relate to Revelation?

9. What is the significance of the candlesticks/lampstands in John's vision of Christ? of the stars in his right hand?

10. What effect would such a vision of Christ have had on John in his situation?

Chapter Three

Letters to the Churches (1)
Revelation 2:1-17

The seven churches of Asia were about to undergo a great testing of their faith in connection with the ordeal of persecution which had already begun near the end of the first century. In the initial vision of the Savior in chapter one of the Apocalypse, he had been seen walking in the midst of these churches. He was there to comfort, encourage, and sustain; he was also there to inspect, warn, and prepare. As Caird expresses it: "Together the letters constitute a visitation of the churches to see whether they are in a fit state to face the coming crisis."

As the resurrected and glorified Christ moved among the seven churches of Asia, he saw many things that encouraged him. He also found some inadequacies and weak points. Thus he wrote to each of the churches for the sake of giving counsel which would suit its situation specifically. It is not difficult to believe that these seven congregations were fairly typical of the churches generally throughout the Roman Empire. If so, this is another element of response to the question "Why these seven and no more?" which was raised in Chapter Two.

Each letter follows a standardized form. First, Jesus is described in terms of some part of the vision of his glory which had been glimpsed in chapter one. In each case, the qualities to which attention is called anticipate some fact about the church being addressed. This is another way of emphasizing his competence to meet every need of his people. Second, an examination of the church is conducted. Both good and bad points are included, and just judgment is given according to the works of the church. Two churches (i.e., Smyrna and Philadelphia) receive only praise from the Lord, while one (i.e., Laodicea) merits only censure. Third, encouragement to faithfulness concludes each letter. Some appropriate appeal is given for the believers to stand fast with Christ and so to be conquerors, and they are urged to hear the voice of the Spirit of God as he encourages them to constancy.

In this chapter and the one to follow, we shall examine each of the seven letters in its turn according to the form just identified. After a brief sketch of the city and a summary of what we know about the origin of the church in it, we will look for Christ's *self-identification* to the church, *his judgment* of the church, and his *appeal* to it.

The Church That Left
Its First Love (2:1-7)

Ephesus was a commercially, politically, and religiously important city of the first century. Standing on the main route from Rome to the east and favored with a good harbor on the Aegean Sea, it was the greatest commercial center in all Asia Minor. Granted the right of self-government by the Romans and given the status of an assize city for the province of Asia, it was here that the most important court cases of the province were heard and justice dispensed by Rome. It was also a great center for religion, for the famous Temple of Diana (Gk, Artemis, Acts 19:23ff) and at least two temples devoted to the worship of the Roman Caesar were situated in it.

Paul came to Ephesus for the first time during his second missionary tour (A.D. 48-51/2). During a weekend visit there, he reasoned with the Jews in their synagogue, made some converts, and left Priscilla and Aquila to carry on the work (Acts 18:18-21). He returned to Ephesus on the third tour (A.D. 52-57) and stayed there longer than at any other single location during his entire preaching career. In the course of a three-year ministry, not only was the church in that great city strengthened but also "all they that dwelt in Asia heard the word of the Lord, both Jews and Greeks" (Acts 19:10; cf.10:31). After Paul's departure, both Timothy (1 Tim. 1:3) and the apostle John labored there.

Christ's Self-Identification

The description Christ gives of himself at the beginning of the letter to the church at Ephesus emphasizes his loving concern for the saints there. "These things saith he that holdeth the seven stars in his right hand, he that walketh in the midst of the seven golden candlesticks" (2:1b). His abiding love for the church at Ephesus will contrast with its diminished love for him.

Christ's Judgment

As the Lord inspected the church, there were several commendable features found. For one thing, the Ephesians were doing many good works; "I know thy works, and thy toil and patience." (2:2a). For another, they were sound in doctrine and opposed to any deviation from the pure Word of God; "I know ... that thou canst not bear evil men, and didst try them that call themselves apostles, and they are not, and didst find them false; ... But this thou hast, that thou hatest the works of the Nicolaitans, which I also hate" (2:2b,6).

In his earlier writings, John had warned of false teachers and indicated the attitude faithful believers were to take toward them (cf. 1 John 4:1; 2 John 9-11). To their credit, the saints at Ephesus had heeded these warnings. The Nicolaitans are singled out as an heretical group which they had repudiated. Although we know very little about the precise nature of this group (cf. 2:15), it is generally believed that the Nicolaitans advocated accommodation of Christianity to its pagan environment; they apparently "engaged in immoral conduct and advocated 'Christian' freedom for all believers so to act" (Beasley-Murray). Also, this church had endured reproach for the sake of Christ. "I know ... thou hast patience and didst bear for my name's sake, and hast not grown weary" (2:3).

There was a serious flaw in the church at Ephesus, however, which threatened to negate all the good things in that church and even to destroy it. "But I have this against thee, that thou didst leave thy first love" (2:4). This church had allowed its early love for Christ and one another to grow cold. It evidently had been a loyal and active church when Paul wrote his epistle to them; its love for Paul is certainly apparent from the record in Acts. By the time of this letter from the Lord, things had changed drastically.

The works of the Ephesians were right, and they were even willing to bear reproach for Christ. But the right motivation for those things was missing. Just here, one should remember the teaching of Paul to the effect that spiritual service rendered without love is without profit for the one performing it (1 Cor. 13:1-3).

This sort of situation must be all too common in every generation. Consider, for example, the person who begins teaching a Bible class or starts to work with a prison ministry out of love and zeal for Christ but who later stays with that project only because nobody else offers to take it up. Does it ever happen? Could it happen with you? Those of us who "grew up in the church" have to be particularly careful in this regard. Do we believe certain doctrines and perform certain deeds out of mere tradition or loyalty to our families? Or are we acting out of personal conviction and sincere love for the Lord?

One wonders how a church could have so many good things said of it and yet have so fundamental a flaw. Mounce has offered the following suggestive comments on this point: "Every virtue carries within itself the seeds of its own destruction. It seems probable that desire for sound teaching and the resulting forthright action taken to exclude all imposters had created a climate of suspicion in which brotherly love could no longer exist. ... Good works and pure doctrine are not adequate substitutes for that rich relationship of mutual love shared by persons who have just experienced the redemptive love of God."

Yes, it is possible for loyalty to the truth to degenerate into rigid orthodoxy; a godly willingness to stand against false teachers can become an ungodly spirit of witch-hunting among brethren. We must defend the faith before the unbelieving world, yet with "meekness and fear" (1 Pet. 3:15). We must oppose a brother who teaches error, yet our stand must be taken "in a spirit of gentleness; looking to thyself, lest thou also be tempted" (Gal. 6:1). By our failure to observe both the spirit as well as the letter of the law of Christ, we have sometimes run people away from the church. May God help us not to repeat the sin of Ephesus!

Christ's Appeal

The Savior attempted to revive the fading love of the Ephesians and to return them to their earlier state of faith and zeal. "Remember therefore whence thou art fallen, and repent and do the first works; or else I come to thee, and will move thy candlestick out of its place, except thou repent" (2:5). He tried to get the Ephesian Christians to recall and contrast their earlier service of love with their present service of ritual; thereby he hoped to use their memory as the lever of repentance to restore them to their first love. Without repentance, the church there would cease to give glory to God and would fail to be a light to the world. The Lord would have to remove its candlestick.

But along with this threat is also found a promise: "He that hath an ear, let him hear what the Spirit saith to the churches. To him that overcometh, to him will I give to eat of the tree of life, which is in the Paradise of God" (2:7).

The Rich Poor Church (2:8-11)

Smyrna was located about forty miles north of Ephesus. A very beautiful city, it was known as the Ornament of Asia. The city still exists as the Turkish city of Izmir and is of great historical interest.

Smyrna had a particularly strong tie to the imperial cult, for as early as 23 B.C. it had built a temple to the emperor Tiberius. When Domitian later began pressing the matter of emperor worship, Smyrna was in the forefront as a pacesetter for all of Asia. As we shall see in the letter to the church there, this put the church in particular jeopardy. Coupled with this loyalty to the imperial cult on the part of the pagans was a large Jewish population. Thus the Christians were in peril from both of these hostile religious groups.

We have no information about the circumstances of the establishment of the church in Smyrna. The first reference to it anywhere in literature available to us is in the Apocalypse. Most probably, it was founded during Paul's extensive ministry centered in Ephesus, during which "all they that dwelt in Asia heard the word of the Lord" (Acts 19:10). Only good is spoken of this faithful church which was about to undergo persecution for "ten days" (i.e., a complete and extensive testing of their faith).

Christ's Self-Identification

"These things saith the first and the last, who was dead, and lived again" (2:8b). With the threat of extreme persecution and even martyrdom (cf. 2:10) over their heads, Jesus identifies himself to these believers as the one who has already overcome death. He assures them that his resurrection is the promise of their own. As a mother might still her anxious child's fear before surgery by telling him "I'll be here when you wake up," so Christ was quieting the anxieties of these saints by telling them that he would be there when they awakened from their ordeal.

Christ's Judgment

His inspection of this church elicited the following: "I know thy tribulation, and thy poverty (but thou art rich), and the blasphemy of them that say they are Jews, and they are not, but are a synagogue of Satan" (2:9).

"Tribulation" (Gk, *thlipsis*) refers to trouble that is especially trying in nature. The "poverty" ascribed to the people of God in opulent Smyrna was certainly material rather than spiritual poverty; in spiritual things, the Lord remarked, the Smyrnian Christians were wealthy. We know that Christianity has always had its largest following among the poor and outcasts of society (cf. 1 Cor 1:26-29). Furthermore, the poverty of some Christians in this city was probably traceable to the fact that the government had confiscated their property and both Jews and pagans had boycotted their businesses. The "blasphemy" (i.e., slander) from the Jews may have been similar to that which Jesus himself had to bear from his own people when they accused him of being in league with Beelzebub (Matt. 10:25). So vile and offensive had the slander from these Jews become that Jesus described them as a "synagogue of Satan."

The Lord had nothing but praise for this church. He knew it was "rich" in faith, love, and courage. This sort of wealth is always to be preferred above material riches, for neither thieves nor inflation can take it from one. Even more, it goes into eternity with its possessor.

Christ's Appeal

The exhortation given to this church is entirely positive in tone. It encourages the saints to hold fast their faith in the face of an intense period of tribulation which was about to come upon them. "Fear not the things which thou art about to suffer: behold, the devil is about to cast some of you into prison, that ye may be tried; and ye shall have tribulation ten days. Be thou faithful unto death, and I will give thee the crown of life. He that hath an ear, let him hear what the Spirit saith to the churches. He that overcometh shall not be hurt of the second death" (2:9-10).

Nothing was hidden from these people. They were told what lay ahead for them and encouraged to prepare for it. In language strongly reminiscent of Matthew 10:28, they were told that those who overcome with Christ – even if their victory, like his, should be through the passageway of death itself – are safe against any future harm from the "second death" (i.e., the lake of fire, cf. Rev. 20: 14).

An interesting sequel to this letter to Smyrna is our knowledge of the martyrdom of one of its members in A.D. 155. Polycarp was burned at the stake in that city for his faith. Told to pay homage to Caesar and to curse Christ, Polycarp told the proconsul, "Eighty and six years have I served Christ, and he hath done me no wrong; how then can I blaspheme my king who saved me?" Threatened with fire, he replied, "Thou threatenest the fire that burns for an hour and in a little while is quenched; for thou knowest not of the fire of the judgment to come, and the fire of the eternal punishment reserved for the ungodly. But why delayest thou? Bring what thou wilt" (Bettenson, pp. 12-16).

Polycarp's response seems to echo the very letter we are studying. Surely its words of encouragement to those who would be faithful unto death must have been imprinted on his heart. Counting back eighty-six years from 155, we arrive at A.D. 69 as the date of his conversion (or, perhaps, birth). So it is altogether possible that he was a member of that body of believers when this letter to Smyrna first reached it from John.

Where Satan's Throne Was (2:12-17)

Pergamum, though not the largest or most important commercial center of Asia, was the capital city of the province. It boasted one of the most famous libraries in the world, with over 200,000 volumes. It was known for its manufacture of parchment. The shrine of Asclepius, the serpent-god who was considered the god of healing by pagans, was located in Pergamum; Charles calls the city "the Lourdes of the Province of Asia" because of its attraction to people from all over the world who came there seeking a cure.

Of greater importance to our study is the fact that Pergamum was the center for emperor worship in Asia. The first temple ever built to Rome and its ruler in Asia was erected there by permission of Augustus in 29 B.C. From that time forward, it was the official center of religious devotion to the empire for the entire region. It is this fact which explains why Pergamum is called by Christ the place "where Satan's throne is." To the degree that this city was the champion of imperial worship, it was appropriate to call it a throne city for Satan. Although we have no direct information about the origin of the church here, we can easily understand that conflict between it and the cult of the emperor was inevitable.

Christ's Self-Identification

To this church, the risen and sovereign Christ appears as "he that hath the sharp two-edged sword" (2:12b). The Word of God which goes forth from the mouth of the Son of Man is authoritative (Matt. 28:18) and powerful (2 Cor. 5:19). As surely as it fights *for* the faithful, it fights *against* the faithless.

Christ's Judgment

"I know where thou dwellest, even where Satan's throne is; and thou holdest fast my name, and didst not deny my faith, even in the days of Antipas my witness, my faithful one, who was killed among you, where Satan dwelleth" (2:13).

The outstanding good quality of this church was its ability to remain faithful to the name of Christ amidst unimaginable pressures to worship the Roman emperor. In fact, of all the seven churches of Asia, this is the only one which is specifically said to have already experienced martyrdom in its midst. An otherwise unidentified brother by the name of Antipas had paid for his faith with his life, but the remainder of the church had held fast to the name of Christ and had not denied the faith under such an intimidating circumstance.

In spite of the general steadfastness of the church in Pergamum, there was a problem in that a few of its members were being allowed to teach a very dangerous doctrine without challenge. "But I have a few things against thee, because thou hast there some that hold the teaching of Balaam, who taught Balak to cast a stumblingblock before the children of Israel, to eat things sacrificed to idols, and to commit fornication. So hast thou also some that hold the teaching of the Nicolaitans in like manner" (2:14-15).

Balaam put a stumblingblock before the children of Israel in their wilderness experience by compromising them with idolatry and seducing them to commit fornication with the daughters of Moab (Num. 22:1-25:5; cf. 31:16). The Balaamites are associated with the Nicolaitans here (cf. 2:6), thus indicating a similarity of view between the two groups. Their common heresy appears to have been that they advocated freedom from all restrictions among the Christians. Whereas Paul had made it clear that one could not "partake of the table of the Lord and of the table of demons" (i.e., worship Christ through the activities of the church and still participate in the pagan festivals and revelries, 1 Cor. 10:21), these false teachers led weak souls to believe that the two systems were not mutually exclusive.

The rebuke of the whole church on this point was due to its lackadaisical attitude toward these false teachers. The church was being too tolerant with them; there was inadequate rebuke of these people and evidently no thought of excluding them from the church's fellowship. Painful as such action may be, it is required of the church when deliberate and unrepented sin is found in the body. "Know ye not that a little leaven leaveneth the whole lump? Purge out the old leaven, that ye may be a new lump, even as ye are unleavened" (1 Cor. 5:6b-7). This counsel of Paul to the church at Corinth certainly fit the situation at Pergamum. Neither Corinth nor Pergamum was taking a firm enough stand against evil within the body. If Ephesus erred by being scrupulously orthodox but unloving, Pergamum erred by its toleration of error in the name of love. In these two extremes is typified a common situation in the church: we are prone to dogmatism in matters where we should exercise tolerance (i.e., matters of judgment and private opinion, Rom. 14) and apt to be lax in matters which call for an unyielding posture (i.e., revealed matters of faith and morals).

Christ's Appeal

The hope held out to these saints was made conditional upon their willingness to deal with the false teachers in their midst. "Repent therefore; or else I come to thee quickly, and I will make war against them with the sword of my mouth. He that hath an ear, let him hear what the Spirit saith to the churches. To him that overcometh, to him will I give of the hidden manna, and I will give him a white stone, and upon the stone a new name written, which no one knoweth but he that receiveth it" (2:16-17).

The one who overcame both the persecutions of Satan and the seductive false teachings warned against at Pergamum would receive "hidden manna" (i.e., spiritual sustenance from God while in the desert of sin), a "white stone" (i.e., a sign of innocence and victory), and a "new name" written on that stone (i.e., a special form of Christ's name to be worn by those who share in his victory over Satan, cf. 3:12).

Thinking Through Chapter Three

1. What is the standardized form for each of the seven letters?

2. Trace the history of the church at Ephesus from Acts.

3. What good things did the Lord find at Ephesus in the course of his inspection? what bad things?

4. Discuss Mounce's comments on the problem at Ephesus.

5. What connection did Smyrna have to the cult of emperor worship?

6. What sort of poverty was the church at Smyrna experiencing? prosperity?

7. Tell the story of Polycarp in your own words. Why is it such an interesting sequel to the letter to Smyrna in the Revelation?

8. Why was Pergamum the place where "Satan's throne" was located?

9. What false doctrine was troubling the church at Pergamum? How does the problem relate to Rev. 2:6?

10. What blessings were to be given the overcomers at Pergamum?

Chapter Four

Letters to the Churches (2)
Revelation 2:18-3:22

The Home of Jezebel (2:18-29)

Thyatira received the longest of the seven letters to the churches of Asia. This might lead one to suppose that this was a large, influential church in Asia's most important city. In fact, Thyatira was rather insignificant in comparison with the other six cities of Asia. Thyatira possessed no great political, cultural, or religious significance. It was established as an armed garrison town to protect the approach to Pergamum, the capital city of Asia. It had a share in the commerce of the province and was distinguished for the skillful manufacture and use of purple dyes.

As with most of the seven churches, we have no certain knowledge of its origin. It may have been established as a result of Paul's extended work in Ephesus (cf. Acts 19:10); another possibility is that it was founded as a result of the conversion of Lydia and her household, traders in purple who were converted by Paul while they were on a business mission to Philippi (Acts 16:11-15). What we do know of the church in Thyatira is that it, like most churches of all times, had both strengths and weaknesses.

Christ's Self-Identification

As this epistle is begun, the Lord presents himself as strong, bold, and capable of dealing with this church's problem in a thorough manner. "These things saith the Son of God, who hath his eyes like a flame of fire, and his feet are like unto burnished brass" (2:18b).

He is the Divine One (i.e., "the Son of God"), knows the secrets of every heart (i.e., "eyes like a flame of fire," cf. Heb. 4:13), and can unleash heaven's wrath upon evildoers (i.e., "feet are like unto burnished brass"). He will shortly rebuke wicked Jezebel and her followers with the full authority of his being.

Christ's Judgment

Before condemning that wicked woman for her sinful ways and damaging influence within the church, the Lord takes due notice of the good side of the church at Thyatira. "I know thy works, and thy love and faith and ministry and patience, and that thy last works are more than the first" (2:19). How unlike Ephesus was the church in Thyatira. Ephesus left her first love; Thyatira's love and good works were still growing.

The problem with this church centered in a wicked woman (i.e., Jezebel) and her influence on some of its members. "Jezebel" is likely a symbolic name for this woman rather than her actual name. Surely no

37

parents would name a girl "Jezebel" or a son "Judas"! But the name was appropriate to apply to her, for she behaved in the manner of the Old Testament personality who opposed the Lord and his righteous ways in Israel (cf. 1 Kings 16:31).

This woman evidently had prominence among the believers, and she called herself a "prophetess" who was being guided by the Spirit to teach and behave as she did. Shades of the modern charismatic movement and its claim to be leading people to tongue-speaking and other supernatural gifts by virtue of a mandate from on high!

All our information indicates that her doctrine was identical to that of the Nicolaitans and Balaamites mentioned earlier in these letters to the seven churches. It was a doctrine of *compromise*. She and her followers were going to the pagan feasts of Thyatira and participating in them. They held that this was all right, so long as they still participated in the worship and work of Christ, too. "In a city whose economic life was dominated by trade guilds in which pagan religious practices had become criteria for membership, the Christian convert would be faced with the problem of compromising his stand at least enough to allow participation in a common meal dedicated to some pagan deity. To reject this accommodation could mean social isolation and economic hardship" (Mounce). Jezebel offered a "solution" for this difficult problem. She held that one could live in both worlds simultaneously. Jesus said it could not be so. The sin of the church was in tolerating this woman's teaching and influence to go unchecked.

Christ's Appeal

"And I gave her time that she should repent; and she willeth not to repent of her fornication. Behold, I cast her into a bed, and they that commit adultery with her into great tribulation, except they repent of her works. And I will kill her children with death; and all the churches shall know that I am he that searcheth the reins and the hearts: and I will give unto each one of you according to your works" (2:21-23). The Lord's stern posture in relation to Jezebel was neither rash nor unjustified. The woman had been given due time to repent of her sinfulness, but she would not. Thus both she and all those who had followed her lead deserved a severe judgment. It would be forthcoming from the Lord.

To the members of the church who were not following Jezebel, the Savior's appeal was this: "But to you I say, to the rest that are in Thyatira, as many as have not this teaching, who know not the deep things of Satan, as they are wont to say; I cast upon you none other burden. Nevertheless that which ye have, hold fast till I come. And he that overcometh, and he that keepeth my works unto the end, to him will I give authority over the nations: and he shall rule them with a rod of iron, as the vessels of a potter are broken to shivers; as I also have received of my Father: and I will give him the morning star. He that hath an ear, let him hear what the Spirit saith to the churches" (2:24-29).

Dealing with Jezebel was this church's most pressing business, thus

Jesus put "none other burden" upon it. But deal with Jezebel it must! For those who would "hold fast" their good works and persevere unto the end, the Lord promised the "morning star." Since Jesus himself is "the bright, the morning star" (Rev. 22:16), this is most likely to be understood as a promise of his presence and blessings in the lives of the faithful. The power of the Christ is set against the wicked, but it sustains and upholds the righteous.

A Dead Church (3:1-6)

Sardis was a city living in the light of its past glories. In the sixth century B.C., it achieved the zenith of its existence under King Croesus. It was situated on Mt. Tmolus, and its acropolis was virtually impregnable; there was only one passage up the acropolis, and it could be guarded easily. It was never stormed successfully by enemies of the city.

It was taken by stealth, however, when the failure to guard the entrance point allowed Cyrus (546 B.C.) and Antiochus (218 B.C.) to capture the city without a serious struggle. A whole city of people allowed their overconfidence to lead to their downfall – not once but *twice* in its history. In A.D. 17, Sardis was devastated by a terrible earthquake. The main part of the city was then moved down onto the plain at the foot of Mt. Tmolus. At the time of the writing of the Apocalypse, it was a city in decline. Sardis was slowly but surely dying.

Again, we know nothing about the history of the church in Sardis. All we know about it is to be gleaned from this epistle. From it we gather that its condition paralleled that of the city in which it was located. Unless it awakened to its true condition, it was going to die.

Christ's Self-Identification

Jesus presented himself to the dying church at Sardis in the following manner: "These things saith he that hath the seven Spirits of God, and the seven stars" (3:1b). The "seven Spirits of God" is a reference to the Holy Spirit, heaven's quickening power (cf. Rom. 8:11; 1 Pet. 3:18). This church was in definite need of such enlivening power! How would it come about that such power could be felt at Sardis? The Word of the Lord would have to be preached there with power and authority. The "seven stars" (i.e., messengers, cf. Rev. 1:20) would have to be the means by which the Spirit's quickening message would be delivered to the churches. Heaven has caused power to be inherent in the gospel and will uphold all those who preach it faithfully.

Christ's Judgment

It is the general pattern of the letters to the seven churches to begin by calling attention to the good things that can be said and then to move on to the problem areas. In this case, however, the Lord goes straight to the point about the status of the body of Sardis. "I know thy works, that thou hast a name that thou livest, and thou art dead" (3:1c).

This church had a "name" or reputation among men, but the judgment of the Lord against it was that it was a dead church. For a church so accustomed to being praised by men, it must have been a tremendous shock to hear such a judgment pronounced.

Notice particularly that Sardis was evidently experiencing no persecution. How could this be, unless the church there had ceased to be evangelistic? A godly, zealous, and evangelistic church will face difficulties when it is attempting to evangelize in a hostile environment of governmental persecution. The church there must have been content simply to hold services for those already in its membership and was stirring no opposition by challenging Jews, pagans, idols, or anything else. Sardis was a peaceful church, if you like the peace of a cemetery!

The only good thing said about this church comes in the form of a compliment directed to a minority of its membership. "But thou hast a few names in Sardis that did not defile their garments: and they shall walk with me in white; for they are worthy" (3:4). Whereas most of the members of the church of God at Sardis had defiled themselves through inactivity, spiritual arrogance, and lack of evangelistic zeal, there were still a few faithful souls who were trying to carry on the work of the Lord there. Those were held to be "worthy" – not of themselves, of course, but by God's grace – to walk with the Lord in garments of pure white.

Christ's Appeal

To the church at large, the Son of Man issued this exhortation: "Be thou watchful, and establish the things that remain, which were ready to die: for I have found no works of thine perfected before my God. Remember therefore how thou hast received and didst hear; and keep it, and repent. If therefore thou shalt not watch, I will come as a thief, and thou shalt not know what hour I will come upon thee" (3:2-3).

Against the background of Sardis' two humiliations at the hands of enemies who took the city by surprise, the church is warned to awaken to its mission. The fire had gone out at Sardis, and only a few sparks remained among the dead coals. If those sparks were fanned by repentance and rededication, the whole could burn brightly again.

Would it be worth the effort to rekindle the fire? Would it be wise to incur persecution by becoming evangelistic in such a hostile environment? "He that overcometh shall thus be arrayed in white garments; and I will in no wise blot his name out of the book of life, and I will confess his name before my Father, and before his angels. He that hath an ear, let him hear what the Spirit saith to the churches" (3:5-6). Repentance among these people would mean a white robe (i.e., a symbol of purity and victory), their names in the Lamb's book of life (i.e., the roll book of the redeemed, cf. Ex. 32:32-33), and their names confessed before the Father (i.e., claimed as belonging to the Lord, cf. Matt. 10:32).

The Church With an Open Door (3:7-13)

Philadelphia was founded in the middle of the second century B.C. by Attalus II. His loyalty to and love for his brother, Eumenes, won him the designation "brother-lover" (Gk, *philadelphos*). Thus the city came to be called Philadelphia, the city of brotherly love. Attalus founded the city as a center for the spread of Greek culture, language, and lifestyle in Lydia and Phrygia. Christ approached the church there with a challenge to missionary work of a higher and grander sort than that which Attalus envisioned.

We know nothing of the circumstances of the founding of the church in Philadelphia. It is one of the two churches of the seven with which no fault is to be found.

Christ's Self-Identification

"These things saith he that is holy, he that is true, he that hath the key of David, he that openeth and none shall shut, and that shutteth and none openeth" (3:7b). In this three-part identification of himself, it is easy enough to catch the significance of the Lord's presentation of himself as "holy" (i.e., divine) and "true" (i.e., truthful). The third element is not quite so obvious but is nonetheless intelligible and impressive.

The "key of David" takes us back to Isaiah 22:22. There Eliakim, the faithful steward of good King Hezekiah, is represented as having the "key of the house of David" and alone had the right to admit supplicants into the presence of the king. His position was somewhat analogous to that of a presidential appointments secretary. One had to go through him to reach the king, for he alone had the right to open or shut the door of access to his presence.

Jesus stands in this special relationship between mankind and deity. "For there is one God, one mediator also between God and men, himself man, Christ Jesus" (1 Tim. 2:5). Or, in the words of Jesus himself, "No one cometh unto the Father, but by me" (John 14:6). It would be his special challenge to the church at Philadelphia to publish the fact of access to God through Jesus Christ and so to become a missionary center for the gospel in all of Asia.

Christ's Judgment

"I know thy works (behold, I have set before thee a door opened, which none can shut), that thou hast a little power, and didst keep my word, and didst not deny my name. Behold, I give of the synagogue of Satan, of them that say they are Jews, and they are not, but do lie; behold, I will make them to come and worship before thy feet, and to know that I have loved thee. Because thou didst keep the word of my patience, I also will keep thee from the hour of trial, that hour which is to come upon the whole world, to try them that dwell upon the earth" (3:8-10).

The "door opened" before this church was one of evangelistic opportunity; that "none can shut" that door was a promise that no power can stand before the Lord's church to defeat its ultimate purpose of glorifying God – even if temporary setbacks (e.g., Rome's persecution of the church) do discourage at times.

In addition to the problems with imperial persecutions, the church at Philadelphia appears to have been experiencing significant opposition from the Jews of their city (i.e., "the synagogue of Satan") as well. In the great hour of trial which lay ahead for the churches of Asia, Jesus promised to be the defender of those who continued faithfully in his word.

Although the Philadelphians might have appeared to have but a "little power" (i.e., limited numbers, money, prominence), they understood that real power came from loyalty to Christ and his powerful word.

Christ's Appeal

The Lord's exhortation to this church has nothing to do with repentance or threats of disaster. It is rather an encouragement to continued faithfulness and a promise of the reward which awaits faithful believers. "I come quickly: hold fast that which thou hast, that no one take thy crown. He that overcometh, I will make him a pillar in the temple of my God, and he shall go out thence no more: and I will write upon him the name of my God, and the name of the city of my God, the new Jerusalem, which cometh down out of heaven from my God, and mine own new name. He that hath an ear, let him hear what the Spirit saith to the churches" (3:11-13).

The exaltation of those who overcome is presented in two ways here. First, the victor will be made a "pillar" in God's temple. This is to say that one who passes through his testing on this earth and keeps faith with his God will henceforth never be threatened again; he will be utterly secure in heaven and "shall go out thence no more." Nobody will fall from heaven, for the complete period of human testing is passed here on earth for human beings. Heaven is a place of reward and rejoicing, not of renewed testing. Second, the victor will have a number of names written upon him. He will bear the very name of God (i.e., the family name of deity), the name of the city of God (i.e., to signify his citizenship therein), and the new name of Jesus himself (i.e., the name of the one by whose blood he has been saved and through whose power he has come to victory).

The Lukewarm Church (3:14-22)

Laodicea was never politically or culturally important to Asia, but it was famous for its wealth. Three Roman roads converged there, making the city wealthy through the commerce which could be generated from such a strategic location. Much wealth came from the sale of soft black wool which was woven there, too. So wealthy was Laodicea that when the city was damaged heavily by an earthquake in A.D. 60, the citizens rebuilt it without any aid from the state. It was a proud, wealthy, and self-sufficient city.

The church there was probably founded by Paul or one of his associates, for we know that he had a personal interest in its welfare and wrote a letter to the brethren there (Col. 4:16).

42

Christ's Self-Identification

The letter opens with this presentation of the Son of God: "These things saith the Amen, the faithful and true witness, the beginning of the creation of God" (3:14b).

"Amen" is a word put at the beginning or end of a statement to emphasize its truthfulness (cf. John 3:3,5). The Christ is a personal "amen" to all of heaven's communications to mankind, a personal assurance of their truthfulness and reliability. Again, he is called "the faithful and true witness." And, finally, he is identified as the "beginning of the creation of God." This means not that he was the first thing created by God but that all created things came to be by virtue of his creative power; a similar statement about his relationship to creation is found in Colossians 1:16 (cf. John 1:3).

Christ's Judgment

Not a single good thing is said about the church at Laodicea. "I know thy works, that thou art neither cold nor hot: I would thou wert cold or hot. So because thou art lukewarm, and neither hot nor cold, I will spew thee out of my mouth" (3:15-16).

Many commentators take the adjective "lukewarm" here to refer to the spiritual sentiment of the Laodiceans – they were neither devoid of religious enthusiasm (i.e., "cold") nor urgent about the faith (i.e., "hot"). Another possibility for interpretation is set forth by Rudwick in an article in *The New Bible Dictionary* (edited by J. D. Douglas) on "Laodicea." He writes: "For all its wealth, the city could produce neither the healing power of hot water, like its neighbor Hierapolis, nor the refreshing power of cold water to be found at Colossae; but merely lukewarm water, useful only as an emetic. The church was charged with a similar uselessness." On the latter view, Christ's judgment here is directed toward the barren works of the Laodiceans rather than the attitude which was behind their deeds. As Mounce observes, this interpretation explains in a satisfactory way why Christ would have preferred the church "cold" rather than "lukewarm."

Why were their works judged barren? The next two verses explain: "Because thou sayest, I am rich, and have gotten riches, and have need of nothing; and knowest not that thou art the wretched one and miserable and poor and blind and naked: I counsel thee to buy of me gold refined by fire, that thou mayest become rich; and white garments, that thou mayest clothe thyself, and that the shame of thy nakedness be not made manifest; and eyesalve to anoint thine eyes, that thou mayest see" (3:17-19). The Laodicean church was proud and smug in its setting of wealth; it judged itself from a totally inadequate perspective. Although it was oblivious to its true spiritual condition, the Lord was not. In his eyes, this church was "the wretched one and miserable and poor and blind and naked."

The only hope for Laodicea was for that church to turn from its smug self-sufficiency to a genuine dependance upon the Lord Jesus. It needed "gold" (i.e., spiritual treasure), "white raiment" (i.e., genuine purity), and "eyesalve" (i.e., curative for their spiritual blindness) which only he could provide.

Christ's Appeal

Might the Laodiceans interpret this stern rebuke so as to feel that their situation was hopeless? Might they feel shut out from divine love? The Lord tells them: "As many as I love, I reprove and chasten: be zealous therefore, and repent. Behold, I stand at the door and knock: if any man hear my voice and open the door, I will come in to him, and will sup with him, and he with me. He that overcometh, I will give to him to sit down with me in my throne, as I also overcame, and sat down with my Father in his throne. He that hath an ear, let him hear what the Spirit saith to the churches" (3:19-22).

This is anything but a harsh and unloving Christ who is exhorting the people of Laodicea. The picture here is a tender and appealing view of the Son of Man who seeks to save, heal, and uplift. He offers victory and glory to anyone who will turn to him.

Conclusion

These seven churches represent a broad spectrum of possibilities. One has nothing good which can be said of it, and two are without reproach. Most have both strengths and weaknesses.

Is it not the same with the local bodies of the Lord's people in any generation? Because this is the case, much is to be learned from a careful study of the epistles to these seven churches. Insights, counsel, warning, and encouragement come to us and challenge us to be more nearly the churches heaven wants us to be at our time in history. We dare not neglect the valuable lessons to be found here.

Thinking Through Chapter Four

1. Identify the woman "Jezebel" who was causing so much trouble at Thyatira.

2. What was the doctrine Jezebel taught?

3. Why was the threat to her so fierce and direct?

4. Show how the condition of the church at Sardis paralleled that of the city in which it was located.

5. What is the only good thing said about the church at Sardis?

6. What is the Old Testament background to the "key of David" imagery in the letter to Philadelphia?

7. Identify the "open door" set before the Philadelphian church.

8. What are the possible meanings of the word "lukewarm" when used to describe the Laodiceans? Which do you favor?

9. What was the hope held before the church at Laodicea?

10. Of the seven churches, which one had nothing good said of it? Which two had no fault found with them?

Chapter Five

The Throne, the Lamb, and the Book

Revelation 4:1-6:17

Through the first three chapters of the Apocalypse, the activity of the book has had to do with scenes on the earth. The risen Lord appeared to John in a vision on Patmos and wrote separate letters to each of the seven churches of Asia. As chapter four begins, however, the majestic voice of the Christ invites John to look behind the scenes of time-bound events on earth to see what is happening in heaven itself.

"After these things I saw, and behold, a door opened in heaven, and the first voice that I heard, a voice as of a trumpet speaking with me, one saying, Come up hither, and I will show thee the things which must come to pass hereafter" (4:1).

As the result of such an invitation, John is going to be privileged to share in the mind of God and to look into the future. He will be allowed to see what lies ahead for the church of his day, what Rome will reap for its sins against the people of God, and the final outcome of the great struggle between the church and the empire of the Caesars. He will see these things not with his physical eyes but with spiritual eyes (i.e., "in the Spirit," 4:2); he will see them in a series of visions given him by the Lord.

From the vantage point of eternity, then, John was allowed to see a different perspective on the troublesome events which were causing such anxiety among the churches. By permission of the Savior, he was allowed to write down what he saw and to communicate it to the churches of his day. These apocalyptic visions were such as to reassure the saints of the ultimate triumph of the faithful and to encourge them not to lose heart in their struggle.

In this chapter we shall study the initial vision John had of the heavenly scene. We shall see the Father securely enthroned in heaven and the worship he receives constantly from creation. We shall witness a moving scene in which a book containing the destiny of mankind is seen in heaven. Finally, we shall rejoice to learn that the Lamb of God (i.e., Jesus Christ) is both worthy and willing to open that book and to make its contents known to humans.

The Throne of the Almighty

"And behold, there was a throne set in heaven, and one sitting upon the throne" (4:2b).

When John was allowed to look behind the scenes of Rome's hatred, persecution, and apparently invincible power which had been unleashed

45

against the saints on earth, the first thing that he noticed was that God's throne was still intact and still occupied by the Almighty.

Caesar might rail against God and claim the right to be worshipped by men, but those actions changed nothing in the eternal scheme of things. The Pharaohs, Nebuchadnezzar, Antiochus, and the Caesars have all claimed supremacy over God's people at various times and have tried to displace him as sovereign of the universe. Against the passing glory of their thrones, there stands the permanent glory and authority of the throne set in heaven.

Can the one seated on the throne be identified with certainty? Yes, for the song of praise which goes up to him is this: "Holy, holy, holy is *the Lord God, the Almighty,* who was and who is and who is to come" (4:8b). This is God the Father on his eternal throne. In the chapter at hand, he is in company with God the Holy Spirit (cf. 4:5b, "the seven Spirits of God") and will be joined in the next chapter by God the Son (cf. 5:6).

John is unable to give any precise description of the Father; he can only describe his radiance. The beauty of his presence reminded John of precious stones, jasper and sardius. Encircling the throne was an emerald-colored rainbow. Although such a rainbow is difficult to imagine, its significance seems clear. Against the background of the rainbow given as a sign to Noah, this rainbow is a reminder of God's covenant-keeping character. He has a covenant with his church, and he will not forget his people in their time of crisis. "Lightnings and voices and thunders" proceeding from the throne created an awe-inspiring sight.

Around the throne John saw twenty-four elders (4:4). This likely represents the bringing together of the redeemed of God's two great covenants with mankind; the twelve Old Testament patriarchs and the twelve New Testament apostles are combined to give us a total of twenty-four elders around the throne of God. They already have their crowns of life (cf. Rev. 2:10) and white robes of victory. Their crowns and robes foreshadow what will be forthcoming to all the faithful of the ages.

Also surrounding the throne were "four living creatures" (4:6-8) who represent in turn wild animals (i.e., lion), domesticated animals (i.e., calf or ox), flying creatures (i.e., eagle), and mankind. All of God's animate creation is thus represented as worshipping him, serving his purposes, and praising him constantly. It is not Rome who rules the world but God! It is not Domitian who elicits praise from every element of creation but the Almighty!

Not only does the handiwork of God's creation praise him constantly (cf. Psa. 19:1), so also do the redeemed from among men join in this ceaseless praise. When the "holy, holy, holy" song of praise is sung, the twenty-four elders join in it and cast down their crowns before him. The casting down of their crowns (4:10) ought not be taken to mean that they hold their gift of eternal life in contempt but that they humbly acknowledge that such life can belong only to the sovereign God on his throne and is theirs by his grace.

46

As the song of praise continues, all nature and the redeemed join together to say: "Worthy art thou, our Lord and our God, to receive the glory and the honor and the power: for thou didst create all things, and because of thy will they were, and were created" (4:11). God receives all the glory, and it is acknowledged in their song that all things exist by his will. If this is so, then the church on earth need not fear that Rome (or any other wicked power) will be able to thwart that divine will.

The Book of Human Destiny

From the general scene of heaven as the Father's throne room, John's attention was captivated by a scroll in the Almighty's hand. Something about it, perhaps the special security (i.e., seven seals) with which its contents were kept from public view, told John and the other observers of the scene that it would be desirable to know what it contained. "And I saw in the right hand of him that sat on the throne a book written within and on the back, close sealed with seven seals. And I saw a strong angel proclaiming with a great voice, Who is worthy to open the book, and to loose the seals thereof?" (5:1-2).

This scroll is the book of the destiny of mankind. In it could be found the fate of the suffering saints, the outcome of Rome's machinations against the church, and an outline of the future from John's time through the resolution of the particular battle raging between his brethren and Satan's forces. The things revealed in the subsequent visions of the Revelation were bound up in this scroll. Was anyone "worthy" to take, open, and reveal its contents?

"And no one in heaven or on the earth, or under the earth, was able to open the book, or to look thereon. And I wept much, because no one was found worthy to open the book, or to look thereon" (5:3-4). No angel, prophet, or saint of ages past was worthy to take the scroll from the Almighty and to open its seals. Would the revelation of "things to come to pass shortly" which had been promised and begun now be ended abruptly? Would the completion of the story be denied John? By no means! God does not tease and taunt. He does not hold out a promise only to pull it back from excited and expectant mortals.

The Lamb Who is Worthy

The only one in heaven or earth worthy to open this important scroll had not yet arrived on the scene or, at least, had not yet come to John's attention. "And one of the elders saith unto me, Weep not; behold, the Lion that is of the tribe of Judah, the Root of David, hath overcome to open the book and the seven seals thereof. And I saw in the midst of the throne and of the four living creatures, and in the midst of the elders, a Lamb standing, as though it had been slain, having seven horns, and seven eyes, which are the seven Spirits of God, sent forth into all the earth. And he came, and he taketh it out of the right hand of him that sat on the throne" (5:5-7).

The Christ seen earlier in the Apocalypse in the manner described in

47

chapter one now appears as "a Lamb standing, as though it had been slain." He is the Lamb of God who takes away the sin of the whole world (cf. John 1:29). He has the marks of sacrificial death still on himself, but he is not dead; he is standing and alive. He also has power (i.e., seven horns) and knowledge (i.e., seven eyes) which work for the benefit of those who trust and follow him. Because of who he is and what he has done, he is the one and only person who is *worthy* (in holiness and authority) to open and reveal the contents of the book of the destiny of mankind.

When he comes onto the stage of this drama, there is no struggle between him and the Father. The Father and the Son are united in purpose and action, and the Son takes the book from the Father's hand in order to proceed with the revelation message which has been promised John.

It is worthwhile to note that whereas Christ as the *Lamb* of God is the motif traced out in greatest detail in the Revelation, he is also represented in verse five as the *Lion* from the tribe of Judah and as the *Root of David*. Both these figures come from the messianic passages of the Old Testament. Judah was called a "lion's whelp" and promised that the scepter would not depart from him until its rightful claimant (i.e., the messianic King) appeared (Gen. 49:9-10); and Isaiah 11:1 anticipates that same kingly figure coming as a "shoot out of the stock of Jesse." With the power of a mighty lion and the authority of a king, Jesus is nevertheless presented in primary fashion as the sacrificial Lamb who atones for sin. Yet, lest anyone should think of him as weak in his representation as a gentle Lamb, we are never to lose sight of the power and authority which he possesses in his royal office.

With the scroll in the Lamb's possession and with the prospect of its contents being revealed anticipated, the living creatures, the twenty-four elders, thousands of angels (5:11), and every created thing (5:13) combined their voices to magnify him. "And they sing a new song, saying, Worthy art thou to take the book, and to open the seals thereof: for thou wast slain, and didst purchase unto God with thy blood men of every tribe, and tongue, and people, and nation, and madest them to be unto our God a kingdom and priests; and they reign upon the earth" (5:9-10). The Lamb and the Father are both worthy of worship. In keeping with the frequent use of the number seven (i.e., perfection) in apocalyptic literature, the Lamb is praised by means of seven expressions. The voice of the angelic host adores him in this song: "Worthy is the Lamb that hath been slain to receive the power, and riches, and wisdom, and might, and honor, and glory, and blessing" (5:12).

The stage has now been set for the first dramatic movement of the Apocalypse. The Father is secure on his throne, the secrets of the destiny of mankind are known to him and under his control, and the Lamb has been judged worthy to reveal certain of those secrets to persons who are interested in knowing the outcome of the church's crisis situation in John's time.

48

The Opening of the Seals

The dramatic movement of chapter six has to do with what happens as the Lamb opens the scroll he received from the Father. The opening of the first four seals follows a set pattern. As each seal is opened in its turn, a voice calls "Come" and a horse and rider appear. This is certainly no ordinary scroll or book. John does not read or hear its contents; he *sees* its contents in a series of visions.

Most students of the Revelation understand the four horses and their riders to represent woes which God sends upon Rome. While this is a plausible view, it seems to leave us with a major question: If these are initial judgments of Rome, why do the martyrs who appear in connection with the fifth seal ask God to begin avenging his cause against that mighty enemy?

Perhaps it is best to see the first four seals in terms of a prediction of increased perils which are yet to befall the Christians in the Roman Empire. After all, the Lord never encouraged his people to naive optimisim; he was always honest about the prospects for suffering which lay ahead for his people. It is more likely that the first four seals show what the church would have to face from Rome before that wicked nation began to feel God's judgments against her. If we understand them this way, the question of the martyrs makes perfectly good sense in context.

When the first seal was opened, a white horse bearing a powerful conqueror came into view (6:1-2). The second revealed a red horse with a rider who caused men to slay one another (6:3-4). The third showed a black horse whose rider had a scale in his hand for the purpose of measuring out precious necessities of foodstuffs to men (6:5-6). The fourth revealed a pale horse whose rider was named Death (6:7-8).

In turn these four symbols signify war, bloodshed, famine, and death. Rome had already "declared war" on the church in John's day, but the bloodshed was only beginning in his time (e.g., only one martyr in the seven churches of Asia to this time). As the conflict intensified, economic pressures would subject many Christians to shortages and even starvation. The end result of these converging forces would be the gorging of Death and Hades. Ruin always follows in the wake of such calamities as conquest, bloodshed, and famine. "And there was given unto them authority over the fourth part of the earth, to kill with the sword, and with famine, and with death, and by the wild beasts of the earth" (6:8b).

With the things about to happen on earth identified by means of the first four seals, the opening of the fifth transports us to heaven again to see the reaction of the martyrs to these intensified persecutions of their brethren still on earth. "And when he opened the fifth seal, I saw underneath the altar the souls of them that had been slain for the word of God, and for the testimony which they held: and they cried with a great voice, saying, How long, O master, the holy and true, dost thou

49

not judge and avenge our blood on them that dwell on the earth?" (6:9-10).

The cry of these martyrs should not be seen as one of angry appeal for revenge, for such a spirit would be unworthy of saints of the Living God. Instead, their cry is for justice and the vindication of God himself –his truth, his cause, his church–among mankind.

Deity's answer to the martyrs comes in two parts. First, they were given white victory robes to wear. Their enemies thought they had defeated these godly people by putting them to death; death had, in fact, granted them entrance into victory, rest, and exaltation. Second, they were assured that God would act to vindicate his church – in his own good time. "And there was given them to each one a white robe; and it was said unto them, that they should rest yet for a little time, until their fellow-servants also and their brethren, who should be killed even as they were, should have fulfilled their course" (6:11).

This is a clear case in Scripture of the "problem of evil" being posed in a most unusual setting. If there is a loving and powerful God who oversees his people, why does he allow them to be subjected to such awful conditions? The answer to that question is not easy to provide in each specific case. We trust God to act rightly in every case and commit ourselves to him to see us through hard times. When the time is right, he will bring it all to a halt and reward his faithful people. At the same time, he will destroy the wicked and their devices. Until that time comes for each suffering saint or church, it is our responsibility to wait and to trust the Lord. In the drama of the Apocalypse, the "How long?" question of 6:10 is not answered in full until the complete overthrow of 19:2 has come about.

When the sixth seal is opened in this unfolding drama (6:12-17), there begins to be predicted the fate of Rome. The "earthquake" motif is common in apocalyptic literature to signify social and political chaos. Certainly the sun turning black and the moon to blood are not to be fulfilled literally. In fact, Peter quoted a prophecy from Joel about the sun being darkened and the moon being turned to blood and claimed that it was being fulfilled on the first Pentecost after the resurrection of Christ from the dead (Acts 2:20). In neither Acts nor Revelation is such language to be taken literally. The Acts reference points to the passing away of a Jewish religious order, and the Revelation reference has its fulfillment in the passing away of the Roman political order.

It is definitely a mistake to take these events to refer to the time and circumstances of the final Judgment of the world. The martyrs under the altar have just been informed (6:11) that the human story is incomplete and more faithful Christians are to be added to the list of martyrs for the faith. The judgment here is *judgment in ongoing events of history,* much like "the Day of the Lord" in the Old Testament prophets. A collapse of order in human affairs is being predicted here. Rome is not going to stand forever and continue to persecute the church without end; God is going to shake the wicked empire to its very foundations and shatter it.

The terror of that time is stressed by the things predicted to accompany Rome's fall: the rolling up of heaven as a scroll, the flight of mountains and islands, and the stark terror felt by all mankind. As Hendriksen observes, the point of this description is not to mark out a series of literal events to be watched for as signs of the end of the world but to indicate the horrible hopelessness of the wicked when God acts in history to overthrow their plans. He says the passage "stresses the terror of the day of wrath for the wicked. The dissolving elements, earthquake, falling stars, etc., add terror to the picture."

One can hardly help noticing at 6:15 that exactly *seven* categories of men are listed: kings, princes, chief-captains, rich, strong, bondman, and freeman. This number encountered so many times in this book says that the judgment upon wicked men will embrace all classes of people. No one will be spared God's wrath who has resisted his holy truth.

Conclusion

The sixth chapter ends by quoting the words of wicked men. When the day of divine wrath comes for them, they will cry out to the rocks and mountains, saying, "Fall on us, and hide us from the face of him that sitteth on the throne, and from the wrath of the Lamb: for the great day of their wrath is come; and who is able to stand?" (6:16-17).

Who is able to stand? Who will be able to endure when the wrath of God is revealed upon the earth against Rome? This question is answered in chapter seven, when heaven acts to mark and shield those who are God's own against the terrible day of wrath ahead.

In summary, then, chapters four, five, and six set the dramatic stage for all that will follow in Revelation. *Is Rome railing against God?* He is still secure on his throne. *Do the saints fear that history is out of control and that the future is unknown and unknowable?* God holds the book of human destiny in his hand, and the Lamb is worthy to open it and to reveal its secrets. *But hasn't the Lamb of God been slain?* Yes, but he is alive again, and he will vindicate his church on earth before the very eyes of its enemies.

What is the enduring message of these chapters for present-day students of Revelation? *God is in control of history, and his people are always under his watchful providence.* To use the words of James Russell Lowell, we may summarize as follows: "Truth forever on the scaffold, Wrong forever on the throne. Behind the dim unknown, Standeth God within the shadow, keeping watch above his own" (from *The Present Crisis*).

In the midst of life's confusion, we sometimes forget that God is in control. Looking only at the horrible things which seem to confront us at every turn here and now, we fail to "look behind the scenes" to the God of all comfort who can sustain us.

John was transported in a vision from his island prison and had the veil of heaven pulled aside for him. He was allowed to glimpse the real situation with the Father, Son, and Holy Spirit in their glory. He was permitted to see their adoration by the entire creation. He was given assurances to pass on to his fellow-sufferers about the divine stability which lay behind the transient power of a wicked and godless enemy. May we not miss the point of such a vision for our own time in history when the things of the kingdom of God seem to be threatened on every hand.

Thinking Through Chapter Five

1. What sort of transition occurs at the start of chapter four?

2. What was the first thing John noticed when he was allowed to see the scene in heaven?

3. Identify the one seated on the throne. How did John describe him?

4. What is the significance of the book which comes into view in this chapter? What does it contain?

5. John said that he was moved to weep by the sight of the book. Why?

6. In what three ways is Christ represented in chapter five? What is the significance of each?

7. The opening of the first four seals reveals four horses and their riders. Identify each.

8. What cry of the martyrs was heard in connection with the fifth seal? What answer is given them?

9. What happened in connection with the opening of the sixth seal?

10. Discuss the last two verses of chapter six.

The 144,000 of God's Israel
Revelation 7:1-17

At the opening of the sixth seal (6:12-17), there occurred a general forecast of the fate of Rome for her attempts to destroy the church. An earthquake, the darkening of the sun, the turning of the moon to blood, and other standard apocalyptic symbols for judgment and overthrow foreshadowed the doom which would befall an impenitent Caesar and his devoted followers.

When the horrible fate of Rome was prefigured in this scene, the cry went up, "The great day of their wrath is come; and *who is able to stand?*" The catastrophe of Rome's fall was to be so terrible that it seemed to anticipate the destruction of all mankind. But it was not to be so. Before the opening of the seventh seal, the Lord showed John how the 144,000 of God's Israel were to be marked for protection against the terrors lying ahead. Thus chapter seven constitutes a sort of parenthesis between the sixth and seventh seals; it is an assurance that *some (i.e., God's faithful saints) will be able to stand in the day of the Lamb's wrath against Rome.*

Just here we should pause to observe that the Apocalypse has three series of sevens: seven seals (6:1-8:1), seven trumpets (8:2-11:19), and seven bowls of divine wrath (15:1-16:21). The seals, trumpets, and bowls are not unrelated to one another; neither do they retell the same story three times. Each leads into the other, with the seventh seal revealing seven trumpets and the seventh trumpet heralding the seven bowls of wrath. A brief overview of this entire progression will help one to understand how this seventh chapter of the Apocalypse contributes to the flow of the action within the total book.

First, the opening of the seven seals shows God's concern over the fate of his church and promises the overthrow of Rome for her persecution of the saints. Second, the sounding of the seven trumpets announces preliminary judgments upon the empire of the Caesars. Even as these are sounded, however, a gracious God is punishing only by measured degrees (i.e., a "third part" of the earth, sea, etc. Rev. 8:7, 9, 10, 11, 12); the purpose of these limited judgments is to warn the wicked and to give them the opportunity of repentance. After the sixth trumpet sounds, it is apparent that Rome has gone beyond the point of return. "And the rest of mankind, who were not killed with these plagues, *repented not of the works of their hands,* that they should not worship demons, and the idols of gold, and of silver, and of brass, and of stone, and of wood; which can neither see, nor hear, nor walk: and *they repented not* of their murders, nor of their sorceries, nor of their fornication, nor of their thefts" (Rev. 9:20-21). Third, with the time of repentance gone for Rome, the sounding of the seventh trumpet leads to the calling forth of angels of vengeance whose task it is to bring complete and final doom to the empire. "And I saw another sign in heaven, great and marvelous, seven angels having seven plagues, which are the last, for in them is finished the wrath of God" (15:1).

In chapter seven, then, heaven is pausing in advance of unleashing its fury on Rome to establish the troubled church against what is about to happen. This chapter is an assurance against its destruction either by its enemies or amidst the tribulation God is about to bring on the evil environment in which it exists.

The Restraining Angels

"After this I saw four angels standing at the four corners of the earth, holding the four winds of the earth, that no wind should blow on the earth, or on the sea, or upon any tree" (7:1).

The "four winds of the earth" referred to in this verse symbolize the punitive wrath of God against wicked men. Destruction by the four winds is a common element in apocalyptic imagery. In fact, even in a non-apocalyptic book like Jeremiah, the wrath of God is represented as a mighty tempest of wind. "Behold, the tempest of Jehovah, even his wrath, is gone forth, yea, a whirling tempest: it shall burst upon the head of the wicked" (Jer. 23:19; cf. 30:23). Thus the scene at hand shows the elements of the universe ready to respond to the pleas of the martyrs to vindicate God's cause on earth and to punish wicked Rome for her persecutions.

Those destructive winds were being held in check by four angels. The four restraining angels are then joined in our drama by a fifth angel who addresses them: "And I saw another angel ascend from the sunrising, having the seal of the living God: and he cried with a great voice to the four angels to whom it was given to hurt the earth and the sea, saying, Hurt not the earth, neither the sea, nor the trees, till we shall have sealed the servants of our God on their foreheads" (7:2-3).

The biblical background to this scene is found in Ezekiel 9. The Almighty was about to punish Jerusalem for its sinfulness. Prior to that event, however, he sent a man with an inkhorn through the city to put an *X* on the foreheads of all those who were innocent of her abominations. "And Jehovah said into him, Go through the midst of the city, through the midst of Jerusalem, and set a mark upon the foreheads of the men that sigh and that cry over all the abominations that are done in the midst thereof" (Ezek. 9:4). Destroyers were then sent through the streets of the city (in a vision) to slay without pity everyone who did not have such a mark.

The angel in chapter seven ordered that the destruction of Rome should be delayed until such time as those who were innocent of her abominations were marked. The purpose of marking them on the forehead was the same as in Ezekiel's vision; they were to be spared the utter desolation which God had in store for the wicked.

Those with the mark of God on their foreheads will be able to stand in the day of terrible calamity ahead. The question of Revelation 6:17 is being answered!

Looking ahead in the Apocalypse, the terrors associated with the sounding of the trumpets are not permitted to come upon those with the mark of God (Rev. 9:4); later still, those with this special seal are standing on Mt. Zion with the conquering Lamb of the Revelation (Rev. 14:1); and as the book closes, they are pictured in a state of eternal bliss in heaven (22:4).

This mark or seal is not a physical sign placed upon every true believer in some literal manner. [Please note that Satan's followers will also be given a special mark in the drama of this book. Cf. Rev. 13:16-17; 14:9; 16:2.] The point of this imagery is simply and obviously that each leader in the great struggle between good and evil knows his followers. Heaven's loyal people are sealed so the punishments of the Apocalypse will not destroy them; Satan's forces are given a seal which will guarantee their having a share in the very same wrath their leader will have to experience.

The 144,000 of Revelation

The total number receiving the seal of God is 144,000. It is composed of 12,000 from each of the twelve tribes of Israel. How is the group to be identified?

Three possibilities come to mind immediately. First, the 144,000 are sometimes regarded as a representation of fleshly Israel or, more frequently, all the saved of Israel under the Old Testament system. Second, some understand it to refer to Jewish Christians about to suffer persecution under Rome. Third, others take it to be a reference to the entire faithful church of God (i.e., New Testament or spiritual Israel) on earth.

The first two possibilities are most unlikely. To show that God had protected his Old Testament people through the perils of a time gone by would not be directly relevant to the flow of the message of the book at this point, and the notion that God still has a special purpose for the fleshly descendants of Abraham contradicts all the New Testament teaches about the basis of acceptance before him (cf. Gal. 5:6).

That these are not the literal twelve tribes of Old Testament Israel seems certain in light of the fact that two tribes (i.e., Dan and Ephraim) are not even named.

As to the idea that the number 144,000 is a cryptic reference to Jewish Christians about to suffer persecution under Rome, such a message would offer little comfort to Gentile believers of John's day. And the church of his time had a larger Gentile population than Jewish membership.

The most reasonable interpretation seems to be that the 144,000 are all those believers – both Jew and Gentile – who would remain faithful to the Lord in the face of the persecutions begun under Domitian. As

Charles has expressed it: "In other words, the 144,000 belong not to the literal but to the spiritual Israel, and are composed of all peoples and nations and languages. From this standpoint the number 144,000 presents no difficulty. It is merely a symbolical and not a definite number."

The number itself is created by squaring twelve and then multiplying it by one thousand (i.e., $12 \times 12 \times 1000$). Since twelve is the number for organized religion in apocalyptic literature and one thousand is the number for completeness and wholeness, this is simply a graphic way to refer to *the totality of the faithful church on earth*. God knows his own, and every loyal Christian will be brought through trials to glory. "Howbeit the firm foundation of God standeth, having this seal, *The Lord knoweth them that are his*" (2 Tim. 2:19a).

The church is often referred to in the New Testament as the Israel of God (cf. Matt. 19:28; Luke 22:30; Rom. 2:29; Gal. 6:16; James 1:1, *et al.*). John has already used this figure in Revelation (2:9; 3:9) and will do so again later on (21:2,12).

It should be noted that the sealing of the saints pictured in this chapter does not guarantee their exemption from physical harm during times of persecution or make it impossible for them to apostatize. It serves these two purposes: (1) it guards them against overbearing trials which could demolish their faith (cf. 1 Cor. 10:13) and (2) guarantees that whatever losses might be sustained by God's people on earth will not affect their heavenly reward to diminish it (cf. 2 Tim. 4:7-8).

Did someone foresee not only an intensification of troubles for the church under Domitian's reign but also the terrors of God which would be unleashed against him and the wicked empire he ruled and ask "Who is able to stand"? Here is the answer! *The Lord's faithful church will endure to its reward by the protection, power, and purpose of God.*

The Great Multitude

"After these things I saw, and behold, a great multitude, which no man could number, out of every nation and of all tribes and peoples and tongues, standing before the throne and before the Lamb, arrayed in white robes, and palms in their hands" (7:9).

The 144,000 are on the earth; the great multitude is in heaven itself (i.e., "standing before the throne"). The 144,000 are the suffering yet faithful saints on the earth; the great multitude in heaven has already overcome and has entered into the blessed state of rest and triumph. They are dressed in white robes and have palms in their hands. Both the white robes and the palms signify triumph. This group is shown as an assurance to the church on earth, for the same God who had seen the great host through its time of trial was now keeping watch over the distressed church of the late first century (cf. Heb. 12:1-3).

The multitude rejoices by acknowledging the source of its victory: "And they cry with a great voice, saying, Salvation unto our God who sitteth on the throne, and unto the Lamb" (7:10). They are safely home but not by their own power. They have been saved not by their merit but by divine grace!

Then, with the chorus of praise to God begun by people redeemed from the earth, the heavenly host of angels surrounding the throne joins in the song. Their worship is evidently prompted by seeing the divine work which has been wrought in bringing humans through trials to glory. "And all the angels were standing round about the throne, and about the elders and the four living creatures; and they fell before the throne on their faces, and worshipped God, saying, Amen: Blessing, and glory, and wisdom, and thanksgiving, and honor, and power, and might, be unto our God for ever and ever. Amen" (7:11-12).

Perhaps you noticed that a total of *seven* qualities are ascribed to God in the song. Each one is preceded by the definite article in Greek; this indicates that the supreme or highest degree of each quality is attributed to God. That there are seven is another play on numbers which is so common in apocalyptic literature.

In order to draw John's attention to the group already introduced at verse nine, one of the twenty-four elders near the throne questioned John as to the identity of those people. "And one of the elders answered, saying unto me, These that are arrayed in the white robes, who are they, and whence came they?" (7:13). The purpose of the question was not information, for their identity was known to all in heaven, but to call attention to the means by which these people had been delivered and saved.

That the elder speaking to John did indeed know the identity of the great multitude is evident in that he answered his own question: "And I say unto him, My Lord thou knowest. And he said to me, These are they that come out of the great tribulation, and they washed their robes, and made them white in the blood of the Lamb. Therefore are they before the throne of God; and they serve him day and night in his temple: and he that sitteth on the throne shall spread his tabernacle over them" (7:14-15).

This is a purged and purified multitude – made clean by the blood of the Lamb! Blood is the only means to atonement, life, and heaven. And although some on earth chose to worship Caesar as Lord and to frequent his temples when they were open, the true and living God is worshipped constantly, "day and night in his temple." In response, he "shall spread his tabernacle" over the redeemed. The tabernacle in the wilderness was a sign of God's presence with the nation of Israel; his presence is so real and immediate to those in heaven that the whole of heaven is represented as being "spread over" or opened out to those there.

For those who have endured "great tribulation" [note: already experienced by these people and not lying ahead at the end of days] and who have remained pure by virtue of the "blood of the Lamb," there are no unsatisfied desires in their glorified state. As God's tabernacle is spread over them, the result is: "They shall hunger no more, neither thirst any more; neither shall the sun strike upon them, nor any heat: for the Lamb that is in the midst of the throne shall be their shepherd, and shall guide them unto fountains of waters of life: and God shall wipe away every tear from their eyes" (7:16-17).

The glories of the redeemed are too wonderful to be described in human language. The best John could do, as the Spirit of God led him to write of heaven, was to use a series of negatives – *no* hunger, *no* thirst, *no* scorching heat. And how is such a perfect bliss possible? The Lamb is the supplier! He is the shepherd. He takes his flock to fountains of waters of life. He brings them so near to the throne itself that God can reach out to wipe away every tear.

Conclusion

As the drama unfolds from this point forward in the book of Revelation, the enemies of the church will come under increasingly severe judgment. First partial and finally total outpourings of divine wrath against wicked and persecuting Rome will be graphically described in the powerful language of an apocalypse.

Chapter seven has assured readers of the Apocalypse that the faithful church will be kept securely in the hand of God through it all. The entirety of the faithful body of Christ (i.e., the 144,000 of spiritual Israel) will stand as all others fall before devastating divine judgment and wrath.

Thinking Through Chapter Six

1. How does the sealing of the 144,000 relate to the sequence of opening the seven seals?

2. What are the three series of sevens in Revelation? How do they relate to one another?

3. Characterize the role of the four restraining angels John saw.

4. How does the vision of Ezekiel (Ezek. 9) relate to the events of the Apocalypse at this point?

5. What was the mark placed on the foreheads of God's people? What purpose was it designed to serve?

6. What three possibilities as to the identity of the 144,000 are identified in this chapter?

7. What is your judgment as to the correct view of the 144,000 of Revelation?

8. Would the mark of God spare his people from all danger? Why not?

9. Who is represented by the great multitude seen in heaven in John's vision? What was their status?

10. How were the people of that great multitude related to the blood of Christ?

Sounding the Seven Trumpets

Revelation 8:1-11:19

Between the opening of the sixth and seventh seals, there was a pause for the sealing of the faithful church against the perils which were to accompany the divine wrath about to come upon Rome. This "interlude" was related in the seventh chapter of Revelation and was the topic of the previous chapter of this book. Now, with that interlude finished and the church assured of God's care through the crisis ahead, it is time to return to the sequence of seals which the Lamb has been opening in our drama. Specifically, it is time for the opening of the seventh and final seal.

In our study of chapters eight through eleven of the Apocalypse, we shall see that the opening of the seventh seal reveals seven angels who have seven trumpets to sound. These trumpets symbolize partial judgments against the wicked empire. At this stage, the judgments are *partial* for the sake of giving Rome the opportunity of repentance and salvation. The prospect of divine wrath is tempered with the hope of mercy.

As with the opening of the seven seals, we shall also observe an interlude between the blowing of the sixth and seventh trumpets. Its nature and purpose will be explained in due course.

Preparation for Sounding

A friend of mine who lived through the experience of having a tornado strike his house once described to me the eerie silence which preceded its arrival. The air became calm, there was a period of silence, and then the tornado bore down on him with all its terrifying power. Something similar to his experience is described in connection with the opening of the seventh seal. "And when he opened the seventh seal, there followed a silence in heaven about the space of half an hour" (8:1). The dramatic silence just before the storm emphasizes the impact of the judgments about to be revealed. The "four winds of the earth" are about to be released against Caesar's world (cf. Rev. 7:1-3).

Seven angels are given seven judgment trumpets to blow (8:2), and another angel added "much incense" to the prayers of the martyrs for God to act to vindicate his cause among men (8:3-4). "And the angel taketh the censer; and he filled it with the fire of the altar, and cast it upon the earth: and there followed thunders, and voices, and lightnings, and an earthquake" (8:5). Does God hear the prayers of his saints upon earth? Does he act in response to their pleas? This scene shows that such questions must be answered affirmatively. The angels stand ready now to sound their trumpets of judgment (8:6).

Heaven is ready to move against the enemies of the church. Again, let it be observed that he will act with restraint and with a desire for Rome's repentance rather than her destruction. These trumpets do not signal final judgments, for only a "third part" is affected by each.

The Sounding of Six Trumpets

The first four trumpets affect the environment. The first (8:7) sends hail, fire, and blood upon the earth to burn up a third of its vegetation; the second (8:8-9) damaged a third part of the sea, the creatures moving in it, and the ships sailing upon it; the third (8:10-11) affected one-third of the land waters to make them bitter and poisonous; and the fourth (8:12) caused a third part of the heavenly bodies to cease to give their light to the earth.

The scene here must not be read, as Morris warns, as though it were "scientific prose." Literal-headedness brought to apocalyptic literature results in nonsense. These first four trumpets symbolize the fact that mankind's sin affects the very planet earth itself (cf. Rom. 8:20) and that part of God's judgment against Rome would involve calamities in nature such as crop failures, the loss of seagoing commerce, etc. As bad as these first four trumpets had been in their sounding, we are told immediately that the worst is yet to come. "And I saw, and I heard an eagle, flying in mid heaven, saying with a great voice, Woe, woe, woe, for them that dwell on the earth, by reason of the other voices of the trumpet of the three angels, who are yet to sound" (8:13).

The final three trumpets are worse than the first four, for they affect not simply man's environment but wicked people directly.

The sounding of the fifth trumpet (9:1-12) reveals one of the most mysterious and frightening scenes of the entire book. When the fifth angel blew his trumpet, a star (i.e., messenger, cf. Rev. 1:20b) came from heaven to earth, "and there was given to him the key of the pit of the abyss." The "abyss" (Gk, *abyssos*) is the abode of demons (Luke 8:31) and the place of preliminary punishment for fallen angels, the beast (Rev. 17:8), and Satan himself (Rev. 20:3). When the messenger opened this horrible pit, the atmosphere was darkened by a thick smoke which issued from it. From the smoke came fierce demon-locusts whose mission was not to eat earth's vegetation but to hurt and torment "such men as have not the seal of God on their foreheads" (cf. 9:4). They were destined to create such anguish among men that their victims would desire death to release them but would not be granted the respite of death (9:5-6).

We must remind ourselves that this is neither an actual creature being described nor – as some dispensationalist interpreters have suggested – a first-century prediction of fighting with helicopter gunships. This is what Beasley-Murray calls "controlled fantasy" which provides a highly imaginative description of divine judgment against Rome. The latter part of verse seven seems to make it clear that whatever affliction is being signified here comes through evil men as its agents. For some extended

60

period of time (i.e., "five months"), humanity will suffer a fate worse than death at the hands of these men. Summers' suggestion is attractive when he says that the vision of the locusts from the abyss "symbolizes the hellish rottenness, the internal decadence in the Roman Empire. One thing which brought about Rome's downfall was a series of corrupt rulers and leaders. Such a spirit of internal rottenness is pictured here as coming from *within* the empire (out of the earth) to work toward her destruction."

This fierce host had a king whose "name in Hebrew is Abaddon, and in the Greek tongue he hath the name Apollyon" (9:11). In their respective languages, both these words mean *destroyer*. Whoever this person is, he is a wrecker of everything fine and holy. Several commentators call attention to the close relationship between the Greek name of this figure (Apollyon) and the name of the Greek god Apollo. Since Domitian claimed that he was divine by virtue of being an incarnation of Apollo, it may be that John was using cryptic language here to identify the (present) leader of the forces about to bring destruction on the world as none other than the emperor of Rome. This interpretation would certainly be consistent with Summers' identification of the locust plague noted above.

At the blowing of the sixth trumpet (9:13-21), a voice from the horns of the golden altar in heaven calls out, "Loose the four angels that are bound at the great river Euphrates" (9:14b). Earlier in the book, we have been told of the prayers being offered at this altar for the vindication of God's cause on earth (cf. Rev. 6:9-10; 8:3-4). Those prayers are being heard and answered! Specifically, four angels (not to be confused with those of Rev. 7:1) release a fierce army of "twice ten thousand times ten thousand" which had been restrained at the Euphrates River. The Euphrates was the eastern boundary of the Roman Empire. Beyond it lay the fierce cavalrymen of the Parthians. The Parthian host had defeated Roman armies at Carrhae in 53 B.C. and at Vologeses in A.D. 62, and Rome felt her greatest sense of insecurity in relation to the possibility of future invasions from that region.

The symbolism of the sixth trumpet was designed to conjure up Rome's fears of the dreaded armies of the eastern border. The prediction here is not necessarily confined to the potential coming of the Parthians but likely denotes the coming of fierce invaders like them who should be feared and dreaded. The fifth trumpet calls attention to Rome's vulnerability because of her own internal corruption; the sixth looks to a series of invasions from outside her borders. The Apocalypse was telling the first-century Christians that such invasions and their havoc to the empire would not be mere chance happenings of history when they began to occur. God would be behind them, using them to punish and break the wicked empire.

The horses ridden by Rome's enemies in this vision breathe out "three plagues" (i.e., fire, smoke, and brimstone) by means of which a third part of the people are killed (9:17-18). Are there such horses with the heads of lions? Whose tails have serpents' heads to sting and hurt men?

Of course not. This is apocalyptic literature, and the writer has the greatest latitude to create images and paint fantastic pictures which will convey a general impression. The general impression being created here is clearly one of unimaginable and horrifying ruin which was to come upon Rome through the breaching of her borders by implacable foes.

Even in his fierce wrath, however, God's mercy shows through in this frightening scene. The destruction is limited to one-third of mankind in the hope that the remaining two-thirds will repent of their evil deeds. "And the rest of mankind, who were not killed with these plagues, repented not of the works of their hands, that they should not worship demons, and the idols of gold, and of silver, and of brass, and of stone, and of wood; which can neither see, nor hear, nor walk: and they repented not of their murders, nor of their sorceries, nor of their fornication, nor of their thefts" (9:20-21). The principal sin of the empire was idolatry; the people of Rome were worshipping the emperor instead of the true God. And, as immorality always goes hand in hand with idolatry, they were given to murders, sorceries, fornication, and thefts.

The sounding of the sixth trumpet reveals that Rome had already gone too far to be saved. Sin has compounded sin, and the hearts of the wicked have become hardened to the point that they are unable to repent. Nothing remains but to unleash the final woe against the evil kingdom of the beast.

Before the sounding of the seventh trumpet (cf. 11:15f), there is an interlude comparable to that between the opening of the sixth and seventh seals. In this interlude God will show to John and to the suffering church on earth what their mission was to be during the time Rome is feeling the full force of divine wrath for its sinfulness. This mission is explained by means of two visions: the episode of the little scroll (10:1-11) and the two witnessess (11:1-14).

The Episode of the Little Scroll

John saw a mighty angel, clothed in heavenly radiance and with authority which spanned earth and sea (10:1-2). When the angel opened his mouth, he spoke "with a great loud voice, as a lion roareth" (10:3). Such a powerful voice (cf. Amos 3:8) would fill people's hearts with fear; it would make them feel a sense of awful foreboding, unless they knew they were in a safe place.

John reported that the angel's cry was accompanied by "seven thunders" and that he was forbidden to write down their message (10:3-4). The sound of thunder is a sound of warning. It gives advance notice of the arrival of a storm and warns people to prepare for its arrival. The refusal of heaven to allow John to write down the message of the seven thunders was simply to impress the fact that God had given ample opportunity for repentance and that he cannot be considered unjust in unleashing his wrath at this point. No more thunderclaps! No more warnings for Rome! No more *delay* in executing God's judgment against that wicked persecutor of his church!

Thus did the angel raise his right hand to heaven and swear by the Almighty "that there shall be *delay no longer:* but in the days of the voice of the seventh angel, when he is about to sound, then is finished the mystery of God, according to the good tidings which he declared to his servants the prophets" (10:6b-7). What is the "mystery" here? Surely it is the purpose of God with regard to the church. God has purposed the church and the bringing of men to salvation in it from eternity; "his servants the prophets" had spoken of this divine purpose incessantly (cf. 1 Pet. 1:10-12). Satan's forces will not be allowed to defeat that purpose in the life of John, in the lives of John's contemporary believers, or in the lives of Christians today.

Now our attention is called to and becomes riveted on an opened scroll which is in the hand of the mighty angel (cf. 10:2). "And the voice which I heard from heaven, I heard it again speaking with me, and saying, Go, take the book which is open in the hand of the angel that standeth upon the sea and upon the earth. And I went unto the angel, saying unto him that he should give me the little book. And he saith unto me, Take it, and eat it up; and it shall make thy belly bitter, but in thy mouth it shall be sweet as honey" (10:8-9). A similar visionary episode takes place in Ezekiel 2:8-3:3. Ezekiel's scroll was "sweet as honey" to his mouth, although it contained words of "lamentations, and mourning, and woe." John's experience was to be of the very same order.

The little scroll contained the judgments of God upon those who had rejected him. It told of lamentations, mourning, and woes against Rome for her sinfulness. It surely told also of the pains and heartaches which Christians would have to endure yet at the hands of that wicked power.

The command was given John, "Take it and eat it up." This refers to the taking, reading, and mastering (i.e., "digesting") the contents of the little book. It was "sweet" in his mouth, because it was an experience of receiving divine revelation; it was "bitter" in his belly, because the woes and denunciations found in it would sadden anyone who believed its message.

What would John's mission be during the time of God's wrath against Rome? What would be his responsibility? "And they say unto me, Thou must prophesy again over many peoples and nations and tongues and kings" (10:11). The message John was receiving was urgent, and all men needed to hear. This he accomplished not only personally (upon his return from exile) but also through the pages of the book we are studying now.

With John's assignment during the coming crisis made clear, the drama moves next to a clarification of the role of the church as a whole during the doom of Rome and the chaos which would attend that event.

The Two Witnesses

At the opening of chapter eleven, John tells of a vision in which he was given a measuring reed and told, "Rise, and measure the temple of God, and the altar, and them that worship therein."

Those who wish to date the Apocalypse in the days of the Neronean persecution of the 60s point to the reference here to the "temple of God" as proof that the temple in Jerusalem was still standing when this book was written. While it is true that this expression originally denoted the Jewish temple (both in certain Old Testament passages and in several New Testament references), it seems unthinkable that the Revelation would have used it of that structure. In the book of Revelation, the Jews are "the synagogue *of Satan*" (Rev. 2:9; 3:9); they are represented as set against the Almighty, the Lamb, and the church. It is the faithful *church* that is the "temple of God" in the Apocalypse (Rev. 3:12). For John, therefore, such an expression could only have reference in this context to the spiritual temple of God, the church (cf. 1 Cor. 3:16; 1 Pet. 2:5). The "court which is without the temple" (11:2) is a symbolic reference to the world of humanity which is outside the body of Christ.

The command for John to "measure" the temple is another way of representing God's purpose to protect and preserve the church against harm. "The meaning apparently is that what is measured at God's command is under the direct control and care of God. The church will be protected in the coming disaster (cf. the sealing of vii. 3). This does not mean that none will perish. There will be martyrs. But the church will not be destroyed" (Morris).

The unmeasured and unprotected outer court (i.e., the world) is given over to sin and thus doomed to eventual destruction. However, there was to be a time during which the people of this outer court would be permitted to abuse – though not destroy – the church: "And the holy city shall they tread under foot forty and two months." The forty-two months is not a literal period of three and one-half years but denotes a time of limited duration. God will not tolerate the trampling of his holy city, the temple, the altar, and his worshippers indefinitely. He will not allow the righteous to experience perpetual persecution without relief.

At this point in the vision, its central point begins to emerge. Heaven gives a charge to "two witnesses" (also called "two olive trees" and "two candlesticks," 11:4) that they are to prophesy in sackcloth during the entire forty-two months (i.e., 1,260 days) that the city and temple of God are being trampled by the nations. The number *two* in apocalyptic literature refers to that which has been strengthened or doubled. Since the candlesticks have been identified already as churches (cf. Rev. 1:20), the two witnesses represent the church in a collective sense.

The two witnesses represent the entire faithful church during the time of the impending ordeal and signify the mission of the church under such a circumstance: *continued faithful preaching of the gospel*. The witnesses are dressed in sackcloth – which indicates mourning and sadness – but they remain loyal to their task. Their prophecies of doom upon God's enemies saddens them; the suffering they endure at the hands of evil men causes them grief; their commitment to the Lamb keeps them at their task through it all! Anyone who dares to oppose their work will suffer the wrath of God as his due reward (11:5-6).

64

Verses seven through ten signify what was to happen to the witnesses after they had accomplished their task of bearing faithful witness to the gospel among sinful men. The "beast" appears from the abyss, makes war against the witnesses, overcomes them, and kills them.

The beast introduced here is even more prominent in the second half (chs. 12-22) of Revelation. He is to be identified with the Roman emperor, and the fact that he "cometh up out of the abyss" signifies his association with the powers of evil. When he kills the two witnesses in this dramatic scene, it appears that he has conquered the church. The witnesses lie in the street, and men rejoice over their death. As Summers observes: "It requires no stretch of the imagination to see this as the attitude of the Roman Empire in this period when it seemed that Christianity was being crushed so that it could never rise again."

All this activity takes place in "the great city, which spiritually is called Sodom and Egypt, where also their Lord was crucified" (11:8). Although some take this to be a reference to Jerusalem (i.e., the city where Jesus was crucified), that city had been destroyed by the time our book was written. *This cryptic reference signifies Rome.* After all, Jesus has been crucified in more places than in just earthly Jerusalem. According to Hebrews 6:6, men "crucify to themselves the Son of God afresh" whenever they give themselves over to sin and harden their hearts against righteousness to the degree that they cannot repent and turn from their sin. The names and memories of past wicked places such as Sodom, Egypt, and Jerusalem are used here to point to the most wicked city of John's day, Rome.

"Tormented" as the empire had been by the faithful preaching of the gospel by the two witnesses, its wicked inhabitants rejoiced at their apparent destruction. But the story is not finished yet!

"And after the three days and a half the breath of life from God entered into [the two witnesses], and they stood upon their feet; and great fear fell upon them that beheld them" (11:11). When it appeared that Rome had conquered the church, it would rise from the ashes of persecution. This sort of coming to the apparent brink of extinction only to come back to vibrant life has occurred more than once in the history of the church. As Rome crumbled, the church survived; and even the enemies of the church would experience "fear" in the knowledge that divine power was behind such a revival. The catching up of the two witnesses into heaven symbolizes the exaltation of those martyrs who died for their faith during the time of Rome's great torment of the church. This will find its complete and ultimate fulfillment, of course, when the saints are caught up to be with the Lord at the time of his bodily return (cf. 1 Thess. 4:17). "But meanwhile it has been partly anticipated in the sight of the world by the tribute paid to the victims of a persecution, sometimes within a few years after their dishonour and death" (Swete).

With the second woe ended (i.e., the sixth trumpet), the time has come for the sounding of the seventh and final trumpet (i.e., the third woe).

The Sounding of the Seventh Trumpet

"And the seventh angel sounded; and there followed great voices in heaven, and they said, The kingdom of the world is become the kingdom of our Lord, and of his Christ: and he shall reign for ever and ever. And the four and twenty elders, who sit before God on their thrones, fell upon their faces and worshipped God, saying, We give thee thanks, O Lord God, the Almighty, who art and who wast; because thou hast taken thy great power, and didst reign. And the nations were wroth, and thy wrath came, and the time of the dead to be judged, and the time to give their reward to thy servants the prophets, and to the saints, and to them that fear thy name, the small and the great; and to destroy them that destroy the earth. And there was opened the temple of God that is in heaven; and there was seen in his temple the ark of his covenant; and there followed lightnings, and voices, and thunders, and an earthquake, and great hail" (11:15-19).

You will recall that there are three series of sevens in the Apocalypse: seven seals, seven trumpets, and seven bowls. In the case of the first two, the seventh in the series reveals the entirety of the series to follow. Thus the opening of the seventh seal introduced the vision of the seven trumpets, and now the sounding of the seventh trumpet opens into the final series of visions in which the seven bowls of the wrath of God are central.

The scenes which begin with chapter twelve concentrate on Satan himself and the overthrow of all his schemes against the people of God. The final series of visions beginning at that point demonstrate that Satan and his allies (i.e., the Roman Empire and its persecuting emperors) do not rule the world but God and his Christ!

Indeed, the voices from heaven proclaim: "The kingdom of this world is become the kingdom of our Lord, and of his Christ: and *he shall reign for ever and ever.*" Jesus Christ was exalted to rule over his people on the first Pentecost following his resurrection from the dead (Acts 2:34-36). He will continue to reign over the kingdom of God until his second coming and the destruction of death at that time (1 Cor. 15:24-28). [Note: In 1 Corinthians 15:28, Paul plainly states that Jesus' rule over the kingdom will *end* at his second coming, when he will deliver up the kingdom to the Father. How, then, can he be said to "reign for ever and ever"? The term "for ever" is often employed in Scripture to refer to an institution or state of affairs which will prevail until some expressed or implied conditions of a covenant are satisfied. Thus, for example, Exodus 12:14 says that the Passover is to be observed "for ever," and Exodus 31:17 indicates the same thing about the sabbath. They were to last until the covenant of which they were a part had accomplished its purpose. Christ's reign over his kingdom will last "for ever" in the sense that it will endure as long as that entity exists on the earth; it will end only when the covenant and state of affairs which have allowed it to exist on earth have been brought to their consummation. Another possibility on this point is suggested by Mounce. He points out that Christ's *singular* reign over the kingdom will end at his second coming but that his *shared* reign with deity through eternity will serve to extend his rule "for ever."]

Verse eighteen indicates the theme about to be developed in the following series of visions: *reward to the faithful saints and destruction of Rome.* Although the language admittedly sounds like a reference to the end of time, the flow of activity in the book has not brought us to that point yet. There are many more events to occur on the earth which are related in chapters twelve through twenty. Thus the rewards and punishments spoken of here are not those of the final Judgment but of the ongoing judgment of God in history to vindicate his own and to defeat the purpose of his enemies.

But hasn't the theme of reward to the saints and punishment for the wicked been developed already in the book? Why go through another round of visions with the same theme?

Yes, this fundamental truth has been revealed already. Earlier in the book, however, it was related with emphasis upon its implications for the church. That God would stand with, give victory to, and sustain his people against their enemies - this encouragement of the saints was the dominant message. Now the story will be told again with a different emphasis. It will speak not of aid to beleagured Christians but of retribution and desolation to their persecutors.

Conclusion

A major point of transition in the book of Revelation has been reached at the conclusion of chapter eleven. The essence of the message of the total book is clear at this juncture: *God is in control of history, and his church is not going to be destroyed by its enemies.*

Beginning with chapter twelve, the terrible details of Rome's final overthrow will be traced in some detail. A new series of characters will be introduced into the apocalyptic drama for the sake of telling the final story. The images will grow more impressive as the message of the book is brought to its final crescendo.

Thinking Through Chapter Seven

1. What is the significance of the seven angels with their trumpets?

2. The first four trumpets affected the environment of mankind. What does this symbolize?

3. The final three trumpets affected wicked people directly. What do they symbolize?

4. What special fears did Rome have in relation to its eastern border? How does the sixth trumpet play on those fears?

5. In the interval between the sixth and seventh trumpets, John had two visions. What were they?

6. What was the message of the seven thunders?

7. The episode with the little scroll has an Old Testament precedent. Identify its significance.

8. Why was John required to "measure the temple of God, and the altar, and them that worship therein"?

9. The vision of the two witnesses has to do with the mission of the church during a time of special trial. What was that mission?

10. What happened when the seventh trumpet was sounded?

Chapter Eight

A Woman, a Child, and a Dragon
Revelation 12:1-17

Revelation's twelfth chapter begins Part Two of the Apocalypse. Part One (chs. 1-11) gives a general overview of the conflict between the church and Rome, assures the church of divine protection through a great ordeal of persecution, and predicts the overthrow of Rome as punishment from heaven. Part Two (chs. 12-22) focuses attention on the sins of the empire and shows just how complete its overthrow will be.

Part One has told about Rome's sins against the church and has offered Rome the opportunity of repentance and salvation from doom and overthrow. The first six trumpets have sounded, and there have been partial judgments against the empire. Its people have not repented of their fornication, their persecution of the saints, and their murderous conduct against the church; if anything, their hearts have been hardened by the initial judgments to the point of being beyond the possibility of repentance. Part Two begins the final movement of the book in order to show that God's wrath against Rome will be "without delay." Having gone too far and having no opportunity now to be spared, Rome faces swift and severe judgment.

The section beginning with chapter twelve was anticipated in the episode of the little scroll two chapters earlier. There John saw a strong angel who had a little book in his hand. A voice from heaven told John to go to the angel and receive the book from him. "And I went unto the angel, saying unto him that he should give me the little book. And he saith unto me, Take it, and eat it up; and it shall make thy belly bitter, but in thy mouth it shall be sweet as honey. And I took the little book out of the angel's hand, and ate it up; and it was in my mouth sweet as honey: and when I had eaten it, my belly was made bitter. And they say unto me, Thou must prophesy again over many peoples and nations and tongues and kings" (Rev. 10:9-11).

The dramatic events of chapters twelve through twenty-two constitute the message of severe judgment which John was obliged to preach to the nations. In other words, the contents of the little book that tasted sweet in his mouth but was bitter to his stomach will be revealed to us in the remaining chapters of the Revelation. The final and complete desolation signified by the seventh trumpet is going to be revealed to John's readers.

The characters in the drama of the Apocalypse are the same in the second half as in the first, although they are represented under new figures. A woman, her children, and the Lamb will be opposed by the dragon and two beasts allied with him. When the conflict finally comes to a close in chapter twenty, the dragon, his allies, and all the evil deeds associated with them will be judged finally and consigned to hell forever. The final state of the redeemed of God will then be pictured at the end of the book; they will be seen safely at home with their Redeemer.

The movement of the action in Part Two of the book is much more rapid than in Part One. At times it occurs at a breathtaking pace and forces us to struggle to keep up with it.

In this chapter, then, we will set the stage for the remainder of the Apocalypse by means of a careful identification of the woman, her child, and the dragon who tries to destroy them.

A Woman With Child

"And a great sign was seen in heaven: a woman arrayed with the sun, and the moon under her feet, and upon her head a crown of twelve stars; and she was with child; and she crieth out, travailing in birth, and in pain to be delivered" (12:1-2).

The imagery of the woman in this chapter calls the reader's mind to the *continuity* between the Old Testament and the New Testament. At times our graphic representations of the relationship between the two major covenants are misleading. We have used three neat circles to indicate three different ages of Bible history. That isn't correct. A straight line of continuity would be better. Instead of three distinct ages, there has been a gradual unfolding of the plan of God. Patriarchy blossomed into the Mosaic Age, and the Mosaic Age gave birth to the Christian religion. They are not so radically discontinuous as we have sometimes represented them.

The imagery of the woman giving birth emphasizes the close relationship we should see between the old and new covenants. The pregnant woman who gives birth in the early part of the chapter is *fleshly Israel*; the woman who flees from her enemies in the latter part of the chapter is *spiritual Israel* (i.e., the church).

The woman is radiant (i.e., arrayed with the sun and moon) with divine revelation. The crown she wears has twelve stars; it calls attention to Israel's twelve patriarchs and twelve tribes. There can be no doubt as to her identity.

Representing Israel as a pregnant woman is not new in Scripture. The figure seems always to suggest the presence of hope, though the hope is usually accompanied with anguish and grief. For example, Micah looked beyond the punishment of Israel and Judah for their sins when he spoke in the eighth century B.C. and pointed to a time when God's kingdom would be established and the Messiah would rule. "Like a woman in travail" (i.e., childbirth pains), Judah would go into captivity in Babylon (Mic. 4:10). But she would be redeemed from that captivity and finally give birth to her child (Mic. 5:3). This is clearly a messianic prophecy in the book of Micah.

Old Testament Israel was always pregnant with messianic hope. She looked forward to the coming of the child of hope and promise whom God had been pointing to from Eden. In fact, she existed as a chosen people for the sake of bringing forth that child of promise. The prophets themselves called attention to the fact that Israel was not chosen by the Lord because of might, wealth, wisdom, or spirituality. That nation was selected by a sovereign act of divine grace and chosen for the single purpose of being the nation through whom God would bless the entire world in the giving of a Deliverer.

In the opening verses of this chapter, this special role of fleshly Israel is set before us again. Israel is great with child, longing to be delivered of the Messiah. *But there is an evil portent on the horizon!*

A Great Dragon

"And there was seen another sign in heaven: and behold, a great red dragon, having seven heads and ten horns, and upon his heads seven diadems. And his tail draweth the third part of the stars of heaven, and did cast them to the earth: and the dragon standeth before the woman that is about to be delivered, that when she is delivered he may devour her child" (12:3-4).

In apocalyptic literature – both biblical and non-biblical – the dragon is probably the commonest of all figures for representing evil. He stands for all that is evil, sinister, destructive, and opposed to God.

There is no difficulty in identifying the dragon seen in John's vision, for verse nine of this same chapter says it is "he that is called the Devil and Satan, the deceiver of the whole world." The dragon is a symbolic representation of Satan and his wicked purpose to defeat heaven's plan to provide a redeemer for humankind. That the dragon is red likely calls attention to the shedding of the blood of martyrs by him. His seven heads and ten horns indicate his great vitality and power. His diadems signify his power to reign over his own. That the dragon's tail can sweep stars from the sky lets us know that he is a formidable adversary.

The dragon stands near the woman about to give birth, and his intention is to "devour her child" when he appears. The brutal imagery is plain. Satan wants to destroy Jesus and his work. Indeed, he has sought to destroy the Messiah from the beginning.

Who can fail to think of the events of the birth of Jesus of Nazareth when reading these lines? Herod the Great learned of the baby who was being born to be King of the Jews. His jealousy for his own position caused him to issue an edict which called for the death of every male child in Bethlehem two years old and under (Matt. 2:16). But it would be a mistake to confine the interpretation of our present chapter to just that event. Everything Satan did during the earthly ministry of Jesus to discourage, thwart, and hinder his work is envisioned here. Surely he thought he had triumphed over him at the cross. He must have rejoiced that he had defeated heaven's purpose.

Satan saw to it that Jesus was rejected by his own, abused by wicked men, and put to death. Little did he know that by means of that very sequence of events he was playing into the hands of God. The greatest vindication of the Messiah would come in connection with his resurrection from the dead by the power of the Holy Spirit.

The Child

"And she was delivered of a son, a man child, who is to rule all the nations with a rod of iron: and her child was caught up unto God, and unto his throne" (12:5).

In these few strokes of his pen, John moves all the way from the entry of the Son of God into the flesh to his ascension. It is all right for him to do that, for his purpose in Revelation is not to give a detailed account of the life and ministry of Jesus on earth. He has done that already in his Gospel.

Here the point is simply that Jesus had an arch-adversary poised and ready to destroy him upon his appearance. The dragon was ready to pounce on the helpless infant! But he did not succeed. Heaven would not allow him to have the victory!

The woman is also given protection from the dragon and his wicked intentions. "And the woman fled into the wilderness, where she hath a place prepared of God, that there they may nourish her a thousand two hundred and threescore days" (12:6). Notice that, whereas the child was caught up to heaven for his protection, the woman is left on earth. She is not left alone and unaided, however. She is given protection and nourishment for the duration of her mission on the earth (cf. Rev. 11:3).

Here the woman is clearly the church (i.e., spiritual Israel) rather than fleshly Israel. Fleshly Israel was participating in the persecution of the church at the time Revelation was written (cf. Rev. 2:9; 3:9). After Christ's appearance and the establishment of the church, there are no special promises remaining to fleshly Israel.

It both astounds and alarms careful students of Scripture to see so much literature produced with the theme that the present-day nation of Israel is the object of Old and New Testament prophecy and that God is working through that nation to bring about his purposes in the world now. *It simply is not true!* God has no promise remaining to Jews after the flesh. "For in Christ Jesus neither circumcision (i.e., belonging to racial Israel) availeth anything, nor uncircumcision (i.e., being a racial Gentile); but faith working through love (i.e., being a Christian)" (Gal. 5:6). The promises of God are not to the fleshly Jews but to spiritual descendants of father Abraham. "For he is not a Jew who is one outwardly; neither is that circumcision which is outward in the flesh: but he is a Jew who is one inwardly; and circumcision is that of the heart, in the spirit not in the letter; whose praise is not of men, but of God" (Rom. 2:28).

Those people whose hearts have been circumcised through baptism (Col. 2:11-12) are the people of God today. Whether Jew or Gentile after the flesh, all people have the same hope in Christ. This is not anti-

Semitism or a statement of political conviction about attitudes toward the nation of Israel; it is simply a theological statement to the effect that it is false to tie any spiritual promise of God or any promise about the future of the church to fleshly Israel. To do so shows a fundamental misunderstanding of the nature of the workings of God in Scripture and history.

Even before he left the earth, Christ promised that the powers of the unseen world would not prevail against the church on earth (Matt. 16:18). Both with regard to his purpose in establishing that church and in the matter of its survival through persecution, Christ gave his word that the church would have heaven's protection.

True enough, the protection provided the church in this drama is in the "wilderness." But she is protected nonetheless! The church exists in a world of sin, persecution, and peril. She survives there with the providence and protection of the Lord of heaven and earth. "Crowns and thrones may perish,/ Kingdoms rise and wane,/ But the church of Jesus/ Constant will remain;/ Gates of hell can never/ 'Gainst that church prevail;/ We have Christ's own promise,/ And that cannot fail." These are the words we sing so often which reflect the Lord's assurances to his church in the wilderness.

In a very impressive manner, the total issue at stake in the universe has been summed up in six verses of this chapter.

War in Heaven

The struggle between good and evil does involve *the entire universe* in its scope. It is a cosmic confrontation between God and all that is holy on the one side and Satan and all that is evil on the other. So now, frustrated in his effort to destroy Christ on the earth, Satan is represented as following him to heaven at his ascension only to be met, defeated, and cast down by Michael and his angels.

"And there was war in heaven: Michael and his angels going forth to war with the dragon; and the dragon warred and his angels; and they prevailed not, neither was their place found any more in heaven. And the great dragon was cast down, the old serpent, he that is called the Devil and Satan, the deceiver of the whole world; he was cast down to the earth, and his angels were cast down with him. And I heard a great voice in heaven, saying, Now is come the salvation, and the power, and the kingdom of our God, and the authority of his Christ: for the accuser of our brethren is cast down, who accuseth them before our God day and night. And they overcame him because of the blood of the Lamb, and because of the word of their testimony; and they loved not their life even unto death. Therefore rejoice, O heavens, and ye that dwell in them. Woe for the earth and for the sea: because the devil is gone down unto you, having great wrath, knowing that he hath but a short time" (12:7-12).

This is no literal recounting of events, and nothing of this sort happened in connection with the resurrection and ascension. Remember, this is *apocalyptic drama*. Neither does this passage relate the origin of Satan, for the drama here is not about the beginning of time and his fall before the creation of the world (cf. 2 Pet. 2:4; Jude 6) but recounts the first-century condition of the church. It is a symbolic representation of Satan's angry reaction to the escape of the Messiah from his wicked plot to destroy him.

As Satan and his unholy army attempt to storm the righteous citadel of heaven, Michael and his fellow angels engage them in battle. Because God is the source of their strength, Michael and his angels prevail and cast the intruders down to earth.

When this conflict was finished, "a great voice" was heard from heaven. Whether it was the voice of a single person or the unified chorus of all who dwell in that holy city is unclear. The language of the song (i.e., "*our* brethren," "*our* God") tends to support the latter view. At any rate, the song ascribes the victory over Satan not to Michael but to the blood of the Lamb (v. 11). Every victory over Satan, sin, and self is by that same power.

In particular, the song seems to point to the victory which some had already won over martyrdom (i.e., "they loved not their life even unto death") and points with assurance to the same victory which others will win. The song is one of confident rejoicing. The victory has already been won by the blood of the Lamb, though many are yet to share in its glory.

At the same time, those joining in the victory song foresee horrors ahead for the saints on earth. They know that a defeated and frustrated Satan will turn his full fury on them. There will be many more martyrs now, for Satan sees that his only remaining hope – having failed to destroy the Christ – is to turn on those who follow him to torment and hurt them. Thus there will be an intensification of persecutions for the people of God who are on earth. "The troubles of the persecuted righteous arise not because Satan is too strong, but because he is beaten. He is doing all the harm he can while he can. But he will not be able to do this for much longer" (Morris).

Turned away from heaven, Satan focuses his full attention and rage on the woman (i.e., the church) back on earth. "And when the dragon saw that he was cast down to the earth, he persecuted the woman that brought forth the man child" (12:13). The persecution of the church on earth is no coincidence but is due to the machinations of Satan.

Against the woman, the dragon issues a flood of evil to carry her away; the Lord's promise remains good, however, and he delivers her. "And there were given to the woman the two wings of the great eagle, that she might fly into the wilderness unto her place, where she is nourished for a time, and times, and half a time, from the face of the serpent. And the serpent cast out of his mouth after the woman water as a river, that he might cause her to be carried away by the stream. And the earth helped the woman, and the earth opened her mouth and swallowed up the river which the dragon cast out of his mouth" (12:14-16).

Satan either does not know, does not believe, or thinks himself powerful enough to defeat the promise of Christ that the powers of the unseen world cannot prevail against his church.

Unable to destroy the church collectively, Satan turns next to try to destroy individual saints. "And the dragon waxed wroth with the woman, and went away to make war with the rest of her seed, that keep the commandments of God, and hold the testimony of Jesus" (12:17).

"The rest of [the woman's] seed" is John's way of referring to the brothers and sisters of the child seen earlier in the chapter. These are faithful Christians who continue keeping God's commandments and holding the testimony of Jesus in the face of determined opposition.

What this part of the vision is designed to say is not difficult to grasp. Each believer must examine himself to make sure he is still following closely in the footsteps of the Savior. Otherwise the chance increases that Satan can reach him and "devour" him. The devil is determined and crafty in his work of destroying souls.

To draw on another New Testament metaphor, think of the church as the flock of God. The flock that stays close together and pulled in close to its shepherd is safe and protected. But what if a sheep begins to straggle a bit or takes a path different from the flock? He forfeits his protection, and the wolves can pounce on him. In the same way, the Christian who straggles or begins going down forbidden paths is jeopardizing his soul. Stay close to the shepherd; remain within the flock; don't jeopardize your security.

Conclusion

In summary, then, chapter twelve has shown the following movements in the new beginning to the Apocalypse.

Satan tried to destroy the Messiah, but could not; God snatched him up to be with him in his throne. Then the devil turned on the church and used the persecution of Jews, Roman rulers, and finally the entire empire as a flood of evil to overwhelm it; that did not work, for the Lord had prepared a place of protection in the wilderness. What Satan is reduced to doing now is trying to pick us off one at a time; even that cannot succeed among those who keep God's commandments and hold fast the testimony of Jesus.

Satan is defeated, and he knows it. But he will not be cast into his hell without taking every other person he can with him.

Thinking Through Chapter Eight

1. How does Part Two of the Apocalypse relate to the episode of the little scroll?

2. Discuss the sense of continuity between the old and new covenants which is implicit in the figure of the pregnant woman.

3. What is the general notion associated with the figure of Israel as a pregnant woman? Where in Scripture is the figure found outside Revelation?

4. A dragon comes on the scene in chapter twelve. Identify it.

5. What role does the dragon play in our drama in its first appearance?

6. Identify the child born of the pregnant woman? How did he escape the dragon?

7. What became of the woman after she had given birth?

8. Who constitutes the "Israel of God" today? Are there biblical promises remaining to fleshly Israel?

9. Discuss the meaning of the dragon's attempt to invade heaven. What was the ultimate outcome of his attempt?

10. What was the primary message of chapter twelve to the original readers of Revelation?

Chapter Nine

The Allies of the Dragon
Revelation 13:1-18

As the second half of the book of Revelation begins, one must be sure to get straight on the list of characters who will be acting out the final drama of the book. In the previous chapter, we identified the woman, her child, a dragon, and the remainder of the woman's children.

In studying chapter twelve, we discovered that *the woman* represents Israel. At the start of the chapter, she is fleshly Israel – pregnant with messianic hope; at the end of the chapter, she is spiritual Israel – suffering persecution in a wilderness environment. The *child* born of her is Jesus, the Messiah who came from the womb of Judaism. The *dragon* waiting to pounce on the child and devour him at his birth is Satan. When that plan was foiled by God's intervention in snatching the child up to heaven, the dragon attempted to storm the gates of glory to defeat the Christ. Cast down from heaven to earth, a frustrated Satan turned his full fury on the woman (i.e., the church) and her other children. Those *other children* are Christian men and women whom Satan tries to destroy one by one. Since he cannot overthrow the church collectively, he will try to break the faith of individual believers as he finds opportunity to tempt and torment them.

In chapter thirteen, we shall meet two additional characters of importance to our drama. "A beast coming up out of the sea" and "another beast coming up out of the earth" will join the dragon and become his allies in making war against the saints of God. The dragon and the two beasts will constitute an unholy trinity for the persecution of the Lamb's followers.

The Beast From the Sea

"And [the dragon] stood upon the sand of the sea. And I saw a beast coming up out of the sea, having ten horns and seven heads, and on his horns ten diadems, and upon his heads names of blasphemy" (13:1).

The dark and mysterious sea was often associated with evil in ancient times. The sea mentioned here is later referred to as "the abyss" (Rev. 17:8). Both terms signify the same thing; they point to the source of evil. The dragon stands on the shore of that awful sea and waits for the appearance of his first ally. A frightening monster appears, and it is clear that he is on the scene to assist Satan in his evil work.

This beast represents Imperial Rome as personified in its emperors. The seven heads are individual emperors of Rome, whose identity will be discussed in more detail in connection with our study of Revelation

77

17:9-10 in Chapter Twelve. The ten horns and their diadems represent the various vassal rulers of kingdoms subject to Rome and through whom its international power was exercised (cf. Rev. 17:12). The name(s) of blasphemy on the heads of this beast point to the divine titles claimed for themselves by various emperors. Recall, for instance, that Domitian required his subjects to speak of him as *dominus et deus* (i.e., Lord and God).

"And the beast which I saw was like unto a leopard, and his feet were as the feet of a bear, and his mouth as the mouth of a lion: and the dragon gave him his power, and his throne, and great authority" (13:2). This beast has fierce powers. Think of the most horrifying features of a leopard, bear, and lion; roll all those terrors into one creature, and the end result is this beast from the sea. Notice that he gets his power, throne, and authority from the dragon. It is Satan who is behind every evil opposition to the work of God in the world. Operating through human agency, he seeks to hinder and destroy all that is righteous and holy. In this case, he was wielding power through the wicked emperors who used Rome's power to persecute and hound the Christians of John's day and beyond.

Satan is ultimately behind every lie that is told, every immoral deed done, and every opposition to righteousness. In the present-day situation we face, both the Lamb and the dragon operate through human agency exclusively. In the first century of the Christian era, angels made earthly visitations, demon possession occurred, and battles were fought with supernatural (i.e., miraculous) powers among men. God is not raising the dead today, and Satan is not possessing individuals against their wills. *The Exorcist, The Omen,* and other similar movies – as well as certain religious groups – would lead people to believe that they must fear Satan's supernatural invasion of their personalities. No, it is much simpler and closer to home than such theories would lead one to believe. The battle for human souls is being fought through human agencies rather than between angels and demons on earth. To the degree that any one of us loves and pursues righteousness, he or she is an agent of God; to the degree that one follows error and practices sin, he or she is a pawn of the devil.

The emperors of Rome did not have supernatural powers – though they did claim such powers, as we shall see later on in the Apocalypse. They had lies, coercion, physical force, bribes, and other seductions to involve people in the unholy things of Satan. The devil is happy to entrust his work on earth to such people, for he knows they will use all their power for his sake.

One of the more arresting and frightening things about this beast from the sea is a wound on one of his heads which looks severe enough to have killed him but from which he has recovered. "And I saw one of his heads as though it had been smitten unto death; and his death-stroke was healed: and the whole earth wondered after the beast" (13:3).

The so-called *Nero redivivus* myth is at the root of this imagery. Nero died by his own hand in A.D. 68, after the Roman senate had condemned him to death. Because he had been so hated among the populace during the last several years of his rule, there was great rejoicing when the word of his death came. But soon the rumor began to circulate that he was not really dead, that he was off in Parthia forming an army and would come against Rome to punish the empire for its repudiation of him. By the end of the first century, the notion that Nero was still alive had faded. It was replaced by the more ridiculous fear among many that he would return from the dead to lead armies against Rome.

Both the present passage and Revelation 17:11 seem to reflect this same background – albeit with a bit of a twist. It is not that the Christian John believed this heathen myth. It is rather that he used a commonly known and generally intelligible myth to communicate to the Christians something of the stark reality of their situation under the successors of wicked Nero. "Nero will indeed return, but reincarnated in a new persecuting emperor, an eighth who is one of the seven (xvii. II)" (Caird).

Nero had led a vicious persecution of the church in and around Rome following the great fire in the capital city in A.D. 64. As these persecutions were revived and widened under subsequent emperors, "the whole earth wondered after the beast." He appeared invincible. Imperial persecutions of the church had ended when Nero died, yet they were being revived in the last decade of the first century. John was in exile, Antipas had been martyred, and the worst was yet to come!

The reaction of the non-Christian world to this renewal of persecution is pictured in this way: "And they worshipped the dragon, because he gave his authority unto the beast; and they worshipped the beast, saying, Who is like unto the beast? and who is able to war with him? and there was given to him a mouth speaking great things and blasphemies; and there was given to him authority to continue forty and two months. And he opened his mouth for blasphemies against God, to blaspheme his name, and his tabernacle, even them that dwell in the heaven. And it was given unto him to make war with the saints, and to overcome them: and there was given to him authority over every tribe and people and tongue and nation" (13:4-7).

This language would not have been appropriate to the limited persecution of the saints under Nero. What he did was limited to Rome and its immediate vicinity. The persecution by this revived beast embraces "every tribe and people and tongue and nation." This is a description of the worldwide persecution under Domitian and his successors; it is the picture of a revival of the tactics of Nero on an even grander scale than he had dared envision.

A clear reference to the cult of emperor worship begun under Domitian is found in the next verse: "And all that dwell on the earth shall worship him, every one whose name hath not been written from the foundation of the world in the book of life of the Lamb that hath been slain" (13:8). Unregenerate people worship the beast. Those whose names are found in the Lamb's "book of life" do not compromise. They have only one deity and yield to only one Lord. To use the language of Paul: "For though there be that are called gods, whether in heaven or on earth; as there are gods many, and lords many; yet to us there is one God, the Father, of whom are all things, and we unto him; and one Lord, Jesus Christ, through whom are all things, and we through him" (1 Cor. 8:5-6).

Although all the emperors since Augustus had been deified by the senate upon their death and entered into the Roman Pantheon, Domitian was the first to take the prerogatives of deity unto himself while still alive. He demanded that statues be erected to him and that subjects of the empire declare their loyalty to Rome by worshipping at his shrine. The Christians would not yield, and Domitian would not exempt them from the requirement. Thus the persecutions began.

A moving admonition to endurance and faithfulness is given in the following words: "If any man hath an ear, let him hear. If any man is for captivity, into captivity he goeth: if any man shall kill with the sword, with the sword he must be killed. Here is the patience and the faith of the saints" (13:9-10).

Many Christians would suffer at the hands of the beast, and some would die. The promise to those hounded saints was to the effect that God's justice would triumph over the beast and his henchmen. Those who have doled out the persecutions (i.e., killed with the sword) will suffer the same fate (i.e., be killed with the sword). God's people entrust their destinies to him and await the divine vindication of their cause; this is their patience [or, more correctly, "patient endurance," cf. NIV] and faith.

How faithful is any Christian to his Lord? How much will he or she endure for the sake of him who endured death for all? It is only in circumstances like these – with a tormenting beast raging against the people of God – that any one of us can know. Peter professed a willingness to die with Christ rather than deny him, yet his faith failed when the test came. The original recipients of Revelation had professed their faith in Jesus. Now they were being warned that many of them would have to prove that faith in the patient endurance of hardships.

As if the dragon and the beast from the sea were not enough for the believers to have to contend with, there is a second beast which arises to make the trio or tormentors complete.

The Beast From the Earth

"And I saw another beast coming up out of the earth; and he had two horns like unto a lamb, and he spake as a dragon. And he exerciseth all the authority of the first beast in his sight. And he maketh the earth and them that dwell therein to worship the first beast, whose death-stroke was healed" (13:11-12). This second beast has the appearance of a lamb (i.e., presents himself as a religious figure), yet he has the voice of a dragon (i.e., speaks lies and damning falsehoods which originate with Satan, cf. John 8:44). His mission is to cause men on earth to worship the beast who has already come up out of the sea (i.e., the empire personified in its emperors).

The original readers of this book would have recognized this character immediately. This is the body of priests which guided and enforced emperor worship throughout the Roman Empire. This beast will later be dubbed the "false prophet" (Rev. 16:13; 19:20). Just as true religion must have its prophets and advocates, so must a false one.

The text then indicates the means this second beast employed in his work of inducing mankind to worship the emperor. For one thing, there were false signs and lying wonders: "And he doeth great signs, that he should even make fire to come down out of heaven upon the earth in the sight of men. And he deceiveth them that dwell on the earth by reason of the signs which it was given him to do in the sight of the beast" (13:13-14a). There is nothing new about the counterfeiting of miracles in connection with false religions (cf. 2 Thess. 2:9). Also, there was the erection of temples and images of the emperor: "Saying to them that dwell on the earth, that they should make an image to the beast who hath the stroke of the sword and lived" (13:14b).

If pseudo-miracles and pompous splendor could not induce some to worship the emperor, there were other means available: "And it was given unto him to give breath to it, even to the image of the beast, that the image of the beast should both speak, and cause that as many as should not worship the image of the beast should be killed" (13:15). Persecution and threats of death would be used against those who resisted emperor worship. The Christians reading these lines from John at the end of the first century would have had no difficulty in identifying what the apostle had in mind.

"And he causeth all, the small and the great, and the rich and the poor, and the free and the bond, that there shall be given them a mark on their right hand, or upon their forehead; and that no man should be able to buy or to sell, save he that hath the mark, even the name of the beast or the number of his name. Here is wisdom. He that hath under-standing, let him count the number of the beast; for it is the number of a man: and his number is Six hundred and sixty and six" (13:16-18).

No single passage in Revelation has stimulated more discussion than this one. *What is the meaning of the mystical number 666?*

Many interpreters of the Apocalypse attempt to decode 666 in order to arrive at the identification of a specific historical individual by means of gematria. This involves assigning numerical values to letters and adding the letters together to derive a number. We know, in fact, that this was a rather popular game in ancient times.

The commonest suggestion made for the solution of this mystery seems to be the name "Nero Caesar." This name is especially appealing against the background of the *Nero redivivus* myth already mentioned. It is true that the Greek name *Neron Kaisar*, when transliterated into Hebrew, yields the number 666. But we are left to wonder why a letter written to Greek Christians in the Roman province of Asia would resort to such a circuitous identification. How likely were the original readers to get the identification right?

Other suggested identifications of the mystery number 666 include Domitian, the pope, Adolf Hitler, *ad infinitum*. Guthrie suggests the key to interpreting this number was known to John's original readers but was lost in subsequent history. Perhaps he is correct.

In light of the mania of so many modern-day interpreters of the Apocalypse to find contemporary persons and events in the book, the following observation by Swete seems particularly appropriate here: "Least probable of all are the attempts of many interpreters to find in the cipher 666 the name of one or another of the conspicuous characters of modern history; such guesses not only are inspired by personal antipathies, but betray ignorance of the real functions of Apocalyptic prophecy."

Far too much has been made of the effort to attach 666 to a specific individual. Recall that in chapter seven a mark or seal was placed on the forehead of God's people to identify them with him and to place them under his authority and protection. Now in chapter thirteen a corresponding mark is placed on those who follow the emperor and look to him for protection. The mark of chapter seven was non-literal in nature and invisible to human eyes. This mark need not be thought of as being different in nature.

John says 666 is the "number of a man" (ASV) or, simply, "man's number" (NIV). Six falls short of perfection (i.e., "seven" in apocalyptic literature); raise anything to its third power (e.g., the "holy, holy, holy" ascribed to God earlier in this book) and it reaches its ultimate. Thus 666 is nothing more nor less than evil raised to its ultimate – evil to the n-th degree! All those who put their trust in mankind generally or any particular human being or human power are opposed to God. They trust human wisdom, human strength, and human works; the saints of God trust only him and his wisdom, power, and workings. This is the fundamental distinction between the lost and the saved in any generation of the history of the world.

Conclusion

The stage is set now for the second half of the book of Revelation. We know who the *heroes* are: the woman (i.e., Israel), the Lamb (i.e., Jesus = the woman's child), the woman's other children (i.e., saints). We also know who the *villains* are: the dragon (i.e., Satan), the beast (i.e., Imperial Rome personified in its emperors), and the false prophet (i.e., the cult of priests who enforce emperor worship).

As surely as the Lord knows his own people (i.e., those with the mark of God on their foreheads), he also knows those who have given themselves over to the arrogant defiance of his will (i.e., those with the mark of the beast).

As the battle is joined between the forces of good and evil, there will be no difficulty in keeping the cast of characters straight. When the triumph of God's cause comes, those who have received the mark of the beast will perish in their rebellion.

Thinking Through Chapter Nine

1. Recall the characters introduced in the previous lesson: the woman, her child, a dragon, and the woman's other children. Identify each.

2. Who is represented by the beast from the sea?

3. How was the beast from the sea related to the dragon?

4. The beast had a wound on one of his heads that looked fatal, yet he was still alive. Relate this to the *Nero redivivus* myth.

5. What was the reaction of mankind to this beast's appearance?

6. A second beast joined the one from the sea. Where did it come from? What does it represent?

7. What role did the second beast play in relation to the first?

8. What are the more frequent theories offered for the meaning of the mystical number 666?

9. What do you think of the proposed solution to the 666 mystery in this chapter?

10. What is the fundamental distinction between the lost and the saved at any given point in history?

Chapter Ten

The Triumphant Lamb
Revelation 14:1-20

God will not allow his righteous cause to be defeated by Satan!
Although they may suffer persecution, they will not be destroyed; although they may have to die for their faith, the eternal life which has been given them as God's free gift will not be taken away from them. This is the message of the book of Revelation in a nutshell.

Yet that message is not presented in so bland and prosaic a fashion as the paragraph above. Revelation presents that message in a very beautiful, very dramatic series of apocalyptic figures. Under the symbolism of a great struggle going on in the cosmos between the Lamb and his followers on the one side and the dragon and his allies on the other, it captivates the imagination and holds the reader's attention.

As the struggle is presented in the Apocalypse, God assures his people as to its ultimate outcome. The purpose of doing so is obvious. He was encouraging the persecuted and discouraged Christians who received the letter originally to stand firm and not lose heart. It is as if he were saying: "Don't give up. Don't think for one moment about giving in to the pressures being brought against you by bowing the knee to Caesar, by proclaiming him Lord, and by compromising your integrity as a Christian. Endure! Be steadfast! The victory belongs to the Lamb and to those who follow him!"

One of the chapters of Revelation designed most directly to call attention to the victory that belongs to the Lamb and his followers is the fourteenth. In summary, chapter twelve showed that Satan could not defeat the Christ of God; chapter thirteen showed who would help Satan in his mission of opposing the work of God in the world. Now chapter fourteen will show the triumph which the Lamb and his allies will share over the dragon and his cohorts.

This section of Revelation is filled with confidence and hope. It is exciting to read and faith-building to study.

The Lamb and the 144,000
"And I saw, and behold, the Lamb standing on the mount Zion, and with him a hundred and forty and four thousand, having his name, and the name of his Father, written on their foreheads" (14:1).

The 144,000 seen with the Lamb in this chapter are the same 144,000 seen already in chapter seven. In the earlier scene, this great host represented the entire faithful church of God under duress on the earth.

Here that body of the redeemed is standing on Mt. Zion with the glorious Lamb. No longer persecuted, the 144,000 are now triumphant.

Mt. Zion may very well represent heaven here, the new Jerusalem which will be described in more detail later. It is more likely intended at this point in the book to signify a *status* (i.e., victory, triumph, vindication) than a place. They have suffered, paid a high price for their faith, and not a few have died as martyrs; but the Lamb has assured their victory through his own triumph, and they are standing with him in security and confidence.

They have the seal of God (i.e., the name of the Lamb and the Father) on their foreheads. This is the mark of identification which was put on the 144,000 back in chapter seven. These are the people who belong to God.

John heard the combined voice of this great multitude singing a "new song" before the throne of God (14:2-3). With a voice as powerful as rushing waters or rolling thunder and as melodious as the sounds of harpers, they sang a song of redemption that "no man could learn ... save the hundred and forty and four thousand, even they that had been purchased out of the earth." Although the angels and living creatures before God's throne had witnessed certain features of human redemption, they had not actually participated in the experience. To be redeemed by the blood of the Lamb is the special prerogative of God's creatures on earth.

Another description of the 144,000 presents them as virgins: "These are they that were not defiled with women; for they are virgins. These are they that follow the Lamb whithersoever he goeth. These were purchased from among men, to be the firstfruits unto God and unto the Lamb" (14:4). This is less a comment on the moral life of the 144,000 than their total spiritual condition. Although fornication as a work of the flesh may have been an issue earlier in Revelation (cf. the letter to the church at Thyatira), here the term is most likely used figuratively of spiritual infidelity.

Spiritual purity is regularly characterized in Scripture as chastity, with impurity and apostasy referred to as adultery (cf. Hos. 4:12; 2 Cor. 11:2; James 4:4). The 144,000 are those who have kept themselves from spiritual adultery. This imagery becomes even more meaningful later in the Apocalypse. The church will be called Christ's bride (Rev. 21:9; cf. Eph. 5:27) and thus distinguished from the great harlot of Revelation 17:1. The pure bride of Christ does not defile herself with the idolatry (i.e., spiritual adultery) of Caesar worship.

These are the people who belong to God. They follow the Lamb wherever he goes. They realize that they have been redeemed by the payment of a great price and are consecrated (i.e., "firstfruits," cf. James 1:18) for heaven's purposes.

Verse five adds the additional information about the 144,000 that their mouths are free of lies and their lives are without blemish. Since they love the one who is himself the Truth (John 14:6), they would not lie by denying him or confessing another instead of him. Thus had they kept themselves free from defilement.

The Lamb is assembling his host of the righteous on Mt. Zion for the final onslaught against Satan, Rome, and all the host of wickedness. Babylon will soon fall, and the dragon, beast, and false prophet will be destroyed. There is no doubt about the outcome of the battle. The Lamb who was slain is alive again, and he stands on Mt. Zion with a perfect number of the redeemed. The victory belongs to him.

Three Angelic Announcements

Now three angels appear in swift succession to announce judgment upon Rome. This does not change the theme from that of the first five verses of the chapter. It simply approaches it from another perspective. The three angelic announcements are further guarantees of the victory of the Lamb over his enemies.

The *first angel* appears to proclaim "eternal good tidings" to all the inhabitants of earth. He cries: "Fear God, and give him glory; for the hour of his judgment is come: and worship him that made the heaven and the earth and sea and fountains of waters" (14:6-7). The hour of divine judgment has come for Rome. This is not the final Judgment Day, the day of the great white throne to be pictured in Revelation twenty. This is judgment against Rome in history's arena, judgment in the form of its doom and dissolution as a political entity.

How can this be called "good tidings" by John? It is to be an event of misery, destruction, and death. Can it be right for the saints to rejoice over such a calamity? It is good news to know that God's purposes will not be defeated in the world; it is good news that God will not allow his righteous cause to be trampled under the feet of sinful people indefinitely. The rejoicing, then, is not over the fact that sinners will perish but that righteousness will triumph. We must never forget that God's wrath is as holy as his love, and both saints and sinners need to know that those who oppose him will not get off.

Then a *second angel* appears and announces: "Fallen, fallen is Babylon the great, that hath made all the nations to drink of the wine of the wrath of her fornication" (14:8). Old Testament Babylon was a place of arrogance and rebellion against God. So wicked and arrogant was that place that God overthrew it completely, so that it has never been rebuilt. The name of that wicked city is attached symbolically to Rome in this book and in many other writings of the Christians in the early centuries of our era (cf. 1 Pet. 5:13).

The reason for Rome's impending fall is specified: she has seduced all nations of the earth to share in her evil ways. By their concessions to idolatry in connection with the worship of Rome's emperor, the nations of her time had chosen to share in her spiritual fornication. [Remember that the 144,000 seen earlier in the chapter had maintained their virginity. They had no part in these wicked fornications.] Now the defiled nations

87

who had not remained free of the pollution of Rome's fornication would be forced to share in her awful fate of suffering divine wrath.

One other thing to notice about this angel's announcement is the certainty of the destruction of Rome. "Fallen, fallen *is* Babylon the great." Although still future at the time of this angel's announcement, the event was so certain that it is spoken of as an accomplished feat. Rome had passed the point of repentance and mercy; it was certain that she could not be spared the fate of divine wrath.

Then comes a *third angel* to announce the fate of all those individuals who have participated in the worship of the emperor of Rome. He says: "If any man worshippeth the beast and his image, and receiveth a mark on his forehead, or upon his hand, he also shall drink of the wine of the wrath of God, which is prepared unmixed in the cup of his anger" (14:9-10a). Those who are not pure, chaste virgins (i.e., all those who have shared in the fornications of Babylon) will drink the wine of God's wrath "unmixed." The Greek word here would be better translated "undiluted." God's straight, undiluted wrath will be poured out for all to drink who have participated in the persecution of the church under Rome's awful leadership. They will reap the fury of heaven's full wrath without mercy.

As to the nature of God's undiluted wrath, there is no doubt. It is described by the angel: "And [anyone who has worshipped the beast] shall be tormented with fire and brimstone in the presence of the holy angels, and in the presence of the Lamb: and the smoke of their torment goeth up for ever and ever; and they have no rest day and night, they that worship the beast and his image, and whoso receiveth the mark of his name" (14:10b-11). No fate worse than this could be imagined. And lest any Christian of John's day should think that compromise with emperor worship would be the easy way out of his predicament (as opposed to martyrdom), John was allowed to reveal the ultimate fate of all those who consent to worship the beast.

The State of the Dead Saints

The Christian's hope is not in finding some form of convenient compromise but in remaining strong and steadfast in the faith. As the third angel expressed it: "Here is the patience of the saints, they that keep the commandments of God, and the faith of Jesus" (14:12). Keeping God's commandments during a time of suffering for righteousness is certainly better than earthly ease followed by eternal torment. How short-sighted we are tempted to be!

Death "in the Lord" is better than whatever type of life one might secure by denying the faith. Thus John writes: "And I heard a voice from heaven saying, Write, Blessed are the dead who die in the Lord from henceforth: yea, saith the Spirit, that they may rest from their labors; for their works follow with them" (14:13). For those persecuted saints to die "in the Lord" would have been for them to die in the faithful performance of their duties to Christ. The expression "in the Lord" is used several times throughout the New Testament. It always means "in harmony with the Lord's will for your life in a designated situation."

Not polluted by Rome's fornications, not compromised by denying the faith, not destined to drink the undiluted cup of God's wrath – blessed are those who stay faithful to their Lord, even if that means death! Such a person receives rest from his labors, and his deeds follow into eternity as part of his reward. These deeds do not go with him for the sake of any merit they have; they go rather as a testimony to the faith he has in Christ (cf. James 2:18) and for the sake of which he was willing both to live and to die.

The Overthrow of Rome

"And I saw, and behold, a white cloud; and on the cloud I saw one sitting like unto a son of man, having on his head a golden crown, and in his hand a sharp sickle. And another angel came out from the temple, crying with a great voice to him that sat on the cloud, Send forth thy sickle, and reap: for the hour to reap is come; for the harvest of the earth is ripe. And he that sat on the cloud cast his sickle upon the earth; and the earth was reaped" (14:14-16).

Again, keep in mind that this is not a scene of the final Judgment but of the judgment that will occur when the announcements of the first three angels have been fulfilled. It is the execution of the wrath of God against Rome for her sins.

Upon a signal received from another angel from the temple of God, the first angel cast his sharp sickle into the earth. Although some students of Revelation identify the angel with a sickle (i.e., "like unto a son of man, having on his head a golden crown") as Christ himself, that identification seems unlikely. For one thing, he already has a clear role in the drama being enacted. He is the Lamb on Mt. Zion with the 144,000 standing near him. For another, the designation "one like a son of man" is rather standard apocalyptic terminology for an angelic being.

When the angel cast his sickle to the earth, the whole earth was reaped. No details of the reaping are given here in the narrative, for those details remain to be told in some detail in the later visions of the Apocalypse.

A second angel of judgment and wrath joins the scene. His mission is to gather the clusters to be cast into the winepress of the Almighty. "And another angel came out from the temple which is in heaven, he also having a sharp sickle. And another angel came out from the altar, he that hath power over fire; and he called with a great voice to him that had the sharp sickle, saying, Send forth thy sharp sickle, and gather the clusters of the vine of the earth; for her grapes are fully ripe. And the angel cast his sickle into the earth, and gathered the vintage of the earth, and cast it into the winepress, the great winepress, of the wrath of God" (14:17-19).

The gathering of a grain harvest (vs. 14-16) and the gathering of the vintage of grapes (vs. 17-20) are not two separate judgments. They are

89

"variations on a single theme" (Caird) and reflect the single event of divine judgment against Rome under dual imagery. It is not a novel thing in Scripture to use dual imagery to describe a single event (cf. Joel 3:13).

That the angel calling for the gathering of the vintage in these verses "came out from the altar" likely means that his action is a final response to the prayers of those under the altar (cf. Rev. 6:9; 8:3-5). In other words, God's actions against Rome are partially in response to the prayers of the martyrs who have pleaded earlier in the book for a vindication of the cause for which they gave their lives on earth.

The scene of the treading of the winepress of the wrath of God is at once both graphic and frightening. "And the winepress was trodden without the city, and there came out blood from the winepress, even unto the bridles of the horses, as far as a thousand and six hundred furlongs" (14:20). It was not wine but blood that flowed from the press as heaven's just judgments came against wicked Rome. When God steps into history to crush his opponents, no sweet juice of the grape flows from that winepress; it is a river of blood.

The river of blood John saw in his vision stretched for 1,600 furlongs (Gk, *stadion* = a Roman measurement equivalent to 607'), or for approximately 184 miles, at a depth reaching a horse's bridle. The number 1,600 may be the product of sixteen (i.e., the square of four = the number of the earth) and 100 (i.e., the square of ten = the number of completeness). Thus the picture seeks to impress the fact that divine judgment "extends to all men everywhere who find themselves beyond the pale of divine protection" (Mounce).

Conclusion

Rome was a vast and powerful empire. From the hindsight of history, we know that its glory has faded. Only the ruins remain. The glory that *was* Rome has perished.

Why did Rome fall? It fell because of her horrible sins against the church. It persecuted the church of the Living God and tried to destroy the faith of saints. The fate of nations as well as individuals is in the hands of our God, and the fate of Rome was a terrible one because of her sin. Rome set itself to destroy the church and was destroyed for her trouble.

But the Lamb triumphs! And all those who stand with him through the difficult times will also stand with him in the day of his triumph! Whether persecuted first-century Christians or pressured modern believers, the promise is good to both. Follow Christ, maintain spiritual purity, allow no lie or denial of the Lamb to pass your lips; you will stand with him in his triumph over Satan and his host.

This is the patience and faith of the saints.

Thinking Through Chapter Ten

1. Where have the 144,000 been seen earlier in Revelation? What change has taken place in their status in the interval?

2. How are the 144,000 described?

3. What was the message of "eternal good tidings" from the first angel?

4. How could a message of disaster be called "good tidings"?

5. What was the message of the second angel?

6. How is the point of the *certainty* of Rome's overthrow stressed in the second angel's announcement?

7. What was the announcement of the third angel?

8. Discuss what is meant by the "patience of the saints" in this context.

9. Describe the event of the reaping of the earth's harvest.

10. What was so unusual about the winepress John saw?

Chapter Eleven

The Bowls of God's Wrath
Revelation 15:1-16:21

All preliminary judgments against Rome have been finished at this point in the Apocalypse, and nothing remains but the execution of God's full wrath against the wicked empire.

There are three series of sevens in the book of Revelation. First, there are the *seven seals* (Rev. 4:1-6:17). They constituted a series of assurances that the church would be protected of God during the time of persecution by Rome. Their primary message was to the effect that God is in control of history and will not allow his people to be destroyed, nor even to be hounded indefinitely. Second, there is a series of *seven trumpets* (Rev. 8:1-11:19). Sounded by seven angels, they have revealed partial judgments (i.e., by thirds) against Rome and contained the possibility of repentance and salvation. Their primary message was that God's holiness is tempered with mercy and even his initial punishments of Rome would be designed to bring about repentance and salvation.

Third, there are *seven bowls of divine wrath* to be poured out on Rome. This series has nothing to do with repeating the messages of the first two series of sevens. The church has been secured against destruction and Rome has been given opportunity to repent. The mighty empire is so arrogant and proud that it will not repent of her evil; she will not cease her persecutions of the church willingly. She has left God no choice but to release the full fury of his wrath against her.

At the start of chapter fifteen, we see "seven angels having seven plagues, which are the last, for in them is finished the wrath of God." In our study of this series of frightening scenes, we shall learn the attitude of God toward all deliberate sin.

A Preliminary Vision

"And I saw another sign in heaven, great and marvelous, seven angels having seven plagues, which are the last, for in them is finished the wrath of God" (15:1). John lets us know that we are nearing the climactic events which will round out the drama of this book and bring down the curtain. Seven angels are holding the "last" plagues of the Apocalypse. Because of Rome's refusal to repent, God has been left with no alternative at this point but to visit his full wrath. When he does so, his wrath is "finished" (i.e., reaches its end) in the final and complete overthrow of the wicked empire.

Not only did John see seven angels with plagues to unloose, he also saw the saints who had died as martyrs of the Roman persecution standing before God. "And I saw as it were a sea of glass mingled with fire; and them that come off victorious from the beast, and from his image, and from the number of his name, standing by the sea of glass having harps of God" (15:2).

Rome had intended to destroy these people. Here they stand in victory! God has brought them through their ordeal, and now they are standing in his very presence. They are occupying themselves in the following way: "And they sing the song of Moses the servant of God, and the song of the Lamb" (15:3a). Moses and Jesus are the two great deliverers of biblical history. Moses led Old Testament Israel out of bondage; Jesus leads New Testament Israel out of her oppression. The song in praise of them must be one with the single theme of *deliverance.*

The part of the song John has recorded in Revelation praises God's mighty and just works in dealing with men and nations according to righteousness. "Great and marvelous are thy works, O Lord God, the Almighty; righteous and true are thy ways, thou King of the ages. Who shall not fear, O Lord, and glorify thy name? for thou only art holy; for all the nations shall come and worship before thee; for thy righteous acts have been made manifest" (15:3b-4).

These martyrs appear to know what the seven angels have in their hands, and they understand the purpose of those plagues. But they are not interceding for God to spare Rome. It simply would not be appropriate at this point in the events of Revelation. So, instead of asking God to delay what they know cannot be postponed (cf. Rev. 10:6), they praise him for his justice which is being exhibited in the wrath about to be poured out.

When they sing "for thou only art holy," they are declaring anew the singular honor which God deserves. It is not the emperor who merits praise and worship but the Almighty. He deserves praise not only for his preservation of the church but also for his overthrow of a nation so wicked as Rome. Even with the limited perspective humans have on history, still we know that evil carries the seeds of its own destruction and that God is not blameworthy for allowing evil deeds to bear their horrible fruits.

Commissioning the Seven Angels

Beginning with verse five, the seven angels holding the final plagues are actually commissioned to pour them onto the earth. "And after these things I saw, and the temple of the tabernacle of the testimony in heaven was opened: and there came out from the temple the seven angels that had the seven plagues, arrayed with precious stone, pure and bright, and girt about their breasts with golden girdles. And one of the four living creatures gave unto the seven angels seven golden bowls full of the wrath of God, who liveth for ever and ever. And the temple was filled with smoke from the glory of God, and from his power; and none was able to enter into the temple, till the seven plagues of the seven angels should be finished" (15:5-8).

94

Calling the seven angels with the seven plagues from the "temple of the tabernacle of the testimony in heaven" underscores the point that Rome's overthrow was to be seen by Christians as a judgment from God and not as a mere accident of history.

The angels are pure and spotless, and they are dressed in beautiful apparel. This indicates the holiness of their mission. Executing God's wrath on evildoers is not an evil task to be undertaken by cruel monsters whose hearts are calloused and whose characters are sadistically warped. Furthermore, one of the four living creatures delivered the seven golden bowls of God's wrath to these angels. Does it seem incredible that wrath should be held in such beautiful containers? The appearance of the angels and the golden bowls to contain God's wrath emphasize a point already made: *God's wrath is as pure as his love.* He does not strike out capriciously. He does not mete out his anger as we impetuous humans do. He executes wrath only after he has given warnings, pleaded with sinful people to repent, and discerned that further efforts to reach them are hopeless. After all, he does not want anyone to perish; he is in the saving business and wants everyone to repent and turn to him for grace (cf. 2 Pet. 3:9).

That no one would be allowed to enter the temple until the seven plagues were finished gives emphasis to their finality. None could come before God to intercede or ask for delay for those about to be punished. The day of Rome's opportunity to be spared has long since gone.

"And I heard a great voice out of the temple, saying to the seven angels, Go ye, and pour out the seven bowls of the wrath of God into the earth" (16:1). Pouring these bowls "into the earth" reminds us that this is not final Judgment at the end of time. It is God's final judgment upon Rome in the ongoing events of history; it is the overthrow of a proud and sinful empire.

With their commission confirmed, the seven angels begin to pour out their bowls quickly. In fact, there may not be enough delay between the bowls to allow the time it takes us to read about their separate effects. In other words, the outpouring was most likely simultaneous; John could only tell about it by identifying the content of each of the seven bowls separately.

As the bowls are poured out, notice what a close resemblance their plagues bear to those visited upon the Egyptians in the Old Testament.

Also, keep in mind that this is apocalyptic imagery. There is no time in history when every non-Christian in the Roman Empire had boils or when all the waters – seas, fresh waters, and cisterns – became blood. These are apocalyptic *symbols* of disaster, suffering, and divine wrath.

Pouring Out the Bowls of Wrath

The *first bowl* affected all people involved in the worship of the beast (cf. Rev. 13:8). Reminiscent of the plague of boils in ancient Egypt (Ex. 9:10ff), "it became a noisome and grievous sore upon the men that had the mark of the beast, and that worshipped his image" (16:2).

The *second bowl* is represented as turning the entire sea to blood and causing everything in it to die (16:3). This plague and the one to follow remind the reader of the Nile River being turned into blood in the days of Moses.

The *third bowl* expands the effects of the second and causes the land waters (i.e., "the rivers and the fountains of waters") to become blood also (16:4). The "angel of the waters" commented on this horrifying event and said, in effect, that men on earth were simply reaping what they had sown. "And I heard the angel of the waters saying, Righteous art thou, who art and who wast, thou Holy One, because thou didst thus judge: for they poured out the blood of saints and prophets, and blood hast thou given them to drink: they are worthy" (16:5-6). Since Rome had spilled the blood of martyrs, they were going to have to drink blood. As surely as the Lamb is "worthy" of the praise of heaven (Rev. 5:9), Rome is worthy of the torment it is receiving under God's judgment.

As if to "amen" the comment of the angel of the waters, the heavenly altar praised God for his true and righteous judgments. "And I heard the altar saying, Yea, O Lord God, the Almighty, true and righteous are thy judgments" (16:7). Earlier in the Apocalypse, the souls under this altar had cried out for vindication (Rev. 6:9; 8:3-5). When judgment comes to those who had been responsible for slaying the martyrs, the very altar itself is represented as replying to praise the event.

The *fourth bowl* has a horrible effect on the sun. "And the fourth poured out his bowl upon the sun; and it was given unto it to scorch men with fire. And men were scorched with great heat: and they blasphemed the name of God who hath the power over these plagues; and they repented not to give him glory" (16:8-9). What a frightening picture of torment upon sinners!

Even though all these calamities of the first four bowls have come in rapid succession, there is not one of the wicked people touched by them that is led to repentance by them. They have gone too far. They cannot repent. Yes, the Bible teaches that people can go so deeply into sin that it is "impossible" for them to repent of their evils (cf. Heb. 6:6). That was the condition of ancient Rome when God began to tear it apart as punishment for its crimes against heaven. So its people did not repent and give God glory for his holiness; they simply added sin to sin by blaspheming his name yet again.

Although the first four bowls affected the earth in general, the *fifth bowl* affects only the beast's throne and his kingdom. "And the fifth poured out his bowl upon the throne of the beast; and his kingdom was darkened; and they gnawed their tongues for pain, and they blasphemed the God of heaven because of their pains and their sores; and they repented not of their works" (16:10-11).

The beast's "throne" is the center of his empire in Rome. That his kingdom was "darkened" simply refers to the weakening and diminishing of Rome's stranglehold on the world. Difficulties of this magnitude might have caused humble men to recognize their errors and repent, but they caused the proud Roman tormenters to compound their sinfulness.

The *sixth bowl* sets the stage for the deafening crash of the empire. "And the sixth poured out his bowl upon the great river, the river Euphrates; and the water thereof was dried up, that the way might be made ready for the kings that come from the sunrising" (16:12). Rome had long regarded the territory across her eastern boundaries (i.e., beyond the Euphrates) as a land of terrible and unknown dangers. Drying up the Euphrates is a way of saying that Rome's worst fears were going to materialize. It signifies that the last obstacle to the fall of Rome has been taken out of the way.

From the mouths of the dragon, beast, and false prophet come "three unclean spirits, as it were frogs" (16:13). The lies and deceptions told by these three unholy allies are represented in a most appropriate manner. These unclean spirits "are spirits of demons, working signs" (cf. 2 Thess. 2:8-12; 1 Tim. 4:1-2) and "go forth unto the kings of the whole world" (16:14a).

For what conceivable purpose are the dragon, beast, and false prophet calling the kings of the earth together? They are summoning them "unto the war of the great day of God, the Almighty" (16:14b). The *Battle of Armageddon* is going to be fought!

Modern-day prophets preach frequently on the Battle of Armageddon. They identify Russia, Israel, the United States, and other parties who are supposed to figure in that great event. They describe a great world war which will lead to the return of the Son of God, the establishment of a kingdom on earth, and his reign from Jerusalem for a thousand years. What fertile imaginations! The Battle of Armageddon isn't ahead of our point in history; it is behind us. It is the apocalyptist's way of describing the final, awful overthrow of the Roman Empire. The battle scene in Revelation sixteen is within the context of the first-century conflict between the church and her archenemy, Rome. The battle was fought in that context, and it does violence to the integrity of the Bible to project it into our time or beyond.

The dragon, beast, and false prophet of the unfolding drama "gathered them together into the place which is called in Hebrew Har-Mageddon (Armageddon, KJV, RSV, NIV)" (16:16). The place named here is identified by a Greek transliteration of the Hebrew *Har-Megiddo* (i.e., the mountain of Megiddo).

Megiddo was indeed a famous battlefield. It was the scene of Sisera's defeat by the power of God through Deborah and Barak (Judg. 5:19-20), of Ahaziah's death at the hands of Jehu (2 Kings 9:27), and of Josiah's untimely death under Pharaoh Necho (2 Kings 23:29). "The last of these events burnt itself into the memory of the Jewish people, and the mourning for Josiah in the valley of Megiddo was long afterwards quoted as a typical instance of national grief (Zech. xii. ll)" (Swete).

Though the *plain* of Megiddo is known as an identifiable place where historical events occurred, there is no geographical location on earth identifiable as the *mountain* of Megiddo. All those modern prophets who anticipate a literal Battle of Armageddon in the Middle East are defying the spirit of apocalyptic literature and missing the point of the Revelation. If it is a literal battle, will it be headed by literal frogs?

The Battle of Armageddon, as envisioned in the Apocalypse, is a symbol for the final overthrow of Rome's evil forces. The name stands for an event, not a place, and signifies the destruction of the terrible enemy which had set itself against Christ and his church in the first century. As Caird puts it: "But, whatever may have been the source or sources of the word *Armageddon*, this much at least is clear, that, like John's other names, it is a symbol. He was not expecting a battle in northern Palestine, but at Rome."

What comfort, assurance, and encouragement would have come to first-century Christians to hear vague news of a battle to be fought nineteen or twenty centuries after their time? They needed to be assured that their present struggle was going to reach a successful conclusion, with the forces of righteousness attaining victory over their foes. The communication of precisely that message is what this chapter – yea, the entire book–of Revelation is about.

Finally, in this connection, notice the parenthetical exhortation of 16:15. "Behold, I come as a thief. Blessed is he that watcheth, and keepeth his garments, lest he walk naked, and they see his shame." With the forces of Satan entrenching themselves for the final and decisive conflict, the Lord injects a note of warning about his coming. Again, the "coming" is not his personal coming at the end of time but in the events of historical judgment against Rome (cf. Rev. 22:20). In effect, Jesus was telling the persecuted people of God: "Christians, before things get any better for you, they are going to get worse! The final cataclysmic battle between the church and mighty Rome is shaping up. You may be tempted to give up and to think the battle a hopeless one, but I assure you that I am coming quickly and swiftly to demolish your adversary. So now is *not* the time to get discouraged. You have resisted Rome and worn the pure garments of faithful discipleship to this point, and you must not yield and stand naked at this final hour of judgment against her. You will forfeit your reason for having lived to this point if you should fail now!"

Then, last in the series, the *seventh bowl* is emptied. "And the seventh poured out his bowl upon the air; and there came forth a great voice out of the temple, from the throne, saying, It is done" (16:17). It is done! It is finished! The final bowl of divine wrath is empty, and everything is ready for the conclusion of the apocalyptic drama relative to Rome.

At that announcement, there were lightnings, voices, and thunders (16:18a); simultaneously, there was a tremendous earthquake "such as was not since there were men upon the earth, so great an earthquake, so mighty" (16:18b). The earth trembled, great cities fell, and Rome herself was divided into three parts (16:19a); even remote islands and mountains were removed by the terrible strains placed on planet earth (16:20). Why? "Babylon the great was remembered in the sight of God, to give unto her the cup of the wine of the fierceness of his wrath" (16:19b). Heaven has taken notice of the sins of Rome and is repaying her justly for her sins. She is having to drink the undiluted cup of divine fury.

"And great hail, every stone about the weight of a talent, cometh down out of heaven upon men: and men blasphemed God because of the plague of the hail; for the plague thereof is exceeding great" (16:21). The scene is one of utter chaos. As the crescendo of wrath comes against Rome, the earth trembles, the Imperial City splits into thirds, and men run frantically to escape the pummeling hail that is falling on their heads to crush them.

As a matter of fact, there was worldwide panic and confusion at the time of Rome's collapse. Greater in magnitude than the awful crash of the stock market in 1929, civilization itself collapsed for a time with the overthrow of Rome. For all her faults and machinations against the church, the Roman Empire was the repository of civilization from the first century B.C. until its collapse in the fifth century A.D. Roman military might had given the world a 200-year period of peace; Roman courts and civil law had given a degree of social stability to the empire which had been unknown previously; transportation and communication had been possible on an unprecedented scale. Civilization was set back for centuries when that empire collapsed and fell.

The Goths entered Italy, captured Rome, and looted the once-impregnable city in 410. In 455, the Vandals plundered the city for two weeks. In 476, the German chief Odoacer deposed the last emperor and nailed the coffin lid on the empire. The world was plunged into the Dark Ages. Sin is so pervasive that not only individuals and families can be ruined by it but even a whole culture or civilization.

Thinking about the devastating consequences of sin for the entire civilized world causes one to reflect about the possibilities for our own time. Might our world become so steeped in sin and rebellion against its Creator that another judgment in history could occur before the great, final Judgment?

Conclusion

The fifth, sixth, and seventh bowls of divine wrath contained Rome's complete and final doom. So momentous is the event of her overthrow in the story of the Apocalypse that its gory details are traced out over four chapters of the book. *Babylon the Great is fallen!*

Thinking Through Chapter Eleven

1. Show how the preliminary vision John saw served to set the stage for the events associated with Rome's catastrophic overthrow.
2. What sort of song was sung by the martyrs in their victory state?
3. How could it be that God's wrath is seen in beautiful bowls of gold?
4. Discuss the similarities between the Old Testament plagues on the Egyptians and the bowls of wrath against Rome.
5. What ironic play on the word "worthy" is made in this context?
6. Describe the effects of the fifth bowl.

7. What was signified by the emptying of the sixth bowl?

8. What is the Battle of Armageddon?

9. Describe the pouring out of the final bowl of divine wrath.

10. From your knowledge of history, what was the worldwide effect of the fifth-century collapse of the Roman Empire?

Chapter Twelve

Babylon the Great is Fallen!

Revelation 17:1-20:10

With the pouring out of the seven bowls of the wrath of God (Rev. 16:2-21), divine judgment against Rome has been pictured in the Apocalypse. That judgment began as a general judgment on that wicked empire (i.e., the first four bowls), but the final three bowls were intended to call particular attention to God's wrath against the capital city itself.

What happens next in the Revelation is something akin to what occurs on your TV screen at times. After a wide-angle shot of some scene, the camera zooms in to catch the details of some part of it. The pouring out of the seven golden bowls of God's wrath was a wide-angle view of his judgment against the sins of Rome. At the beginning of chapter seventeen, we zoom in to see the details of what that judgment does to the Imperial City and to all who depend on her.

Chapters seventeen and eighteen show the fall of Rome under the symbolism of a great harlot being punished for her immoralities. Revelation 19:1-10 shows the rejoicing of the redeemed over Rome's fall. And Revelation 19:11-20:10 pictures the final fate of the dragon, the beast, and the false prophet who have withstood God throughout this apocalyptic drama.

Taken together, the four chapters to be studied now show how complete and devastating the overthrow of Babylon was to be.

A Vision of the Great Harlot

One of the seven angels of wrath invited John to come with him for a closer inspection of the fate befalling Babylon (i.e., Rome). "Come hither, I will show thee the judgment of the great harlot that sitteth upon many waters; with whom the kings of the earth committed fornication, and they that dwell in the earth were made drunken with the wine of her fornication" (17:1-2).

This awful harlot stands in stark contrast with the pure bride of Christ. There can be no mistake as to her identity in the context of the Revelation. First, she is Babylon (17:5; cf. Rev. 16:19). Second, she is "drunken with the blood of the saints, and with the blood of the martyrs of Jesus" (17:6). Third, she is "the great city, which reigneth over the kings of the earth (17:18). All of these descriptions let us know that this is the Imperial City itself, the city where the beast (i.e., emperor) is worshipped and from which have gone out orders to persecute the saints of God.

The kings of the earth had committed fornication with her (17:2) through their economic, military, cultural, and, especially, religious alliances with Rome. This wicked woman is about to be punished for her seductions and immoralities. We have already seen that fornication is often used in Scripture as a symbol for idolatry and spiritual apostasy (Nah. 3:1-4; Isa. 23:15; Jer. 3; cf. Rev. 14:8). Its use here is certainly consistent with that motif. Rome's worship of her emperor and her exaltation of him to the place which belongs to the true God alone was idolatry of the grossest sort (cf. 2 Thess. 2:3-4). Those actions certainly qualified her to be represented as a great *harlot* seducing the nations of the world with her fornications.

In one sense, she sat "upon many waters" (i.e., held sway over many people and was secure, 17:1b); in another, she dwelled in a "wilderness" (i.e., was desolated, 17:3a).

When John was allowed to see this vision of Rome, the woman was "sitting upon a scarlet-colored beast, full of names of blasphemy, having seven heads and ten horns" (17:3b). The beast of Revelation is not a new figure; he has been seen already and was identified as Rome personified in its emperors (cf. Rev. 13:1-10). The picture of the harlot sitting upon the beast reminds us that the city of Rome owed its position to the emperor as head of the powerful Roman state.

The great harlot is described by John with these words: "And the woman was arrayed in purple and scarlet, and decked with gold and precious stone and pearls, having in her hand a golden cup full of abominations, even the unclean things of her fornication, and upon her forehead a name written, MYSTERY, BABYLON THE GREAT, THE MOTHER OF THE HARLOTS AND OF THE ABOMINATIONS OF THE EARTH. And I saw the woman drunken with the blood of the saints, and with the blood of the martyrs of Jesus. And when I saw her, I wondered with a great wonder" (17:4-6). Her dress and jewelry indicate her wealth and splendor. The golden cup from which she drank was loved by her but seen as an abomination by John; it contained the intoxicating history of her persecutions of the church.

She had her name written on her forehead. Charles says it was characteristic of the prostitutes of Rome at this time in history to have their names tattooed or branded on their foreheads. The form of the name she wore indicated that her evils were great enough to have compromised many more than just herself.

At this point in the story, the angel who carried John to see this vision of the wicked woman paused to explain certain parts of it to him. In particular, he focused on the identity of the beast. That the beast "was, and is not; and is about to come up out of the abyss, and to go into perdition" points us back to Revelation 13:3. This is a symbolic representation of the history of the Roman emperors in relation to the church. That the beast *was* likely points to the past persecutions initiated by Nero; yet Nero himself *is not* any longer, for he died and the harm he was doing the church subsided. The beast *is about to come up out of the abyss* and make one last-ditch stand against God's work in the world (cf. Rev. 16:13-14); yet his fate is sealed, and he is destined *to go into perdition.*

The seven heads of the beast (17:7-11) represent both the "seven mountains" on which Rome was built and "seven kings" of the empire. It is highly doubtful that the seven kings can be identified by name; the numeral seven may simply represent the totality of the power personified in the emperor. The statement that "the five are fallen, the one is, the other is not yet come; and when he cometh, he must continue a little while" probably reflects the *Nero redivivus* myth again. Verse eleven says: "And the beast that was, and is not, is himself also an eighth, and is of the seven; and he goeth into perdition." As confusing as this sounds to our ears, unaccustomed to apocalyptic language, it may well have conveyed the following to those who first read it: Nero is one of the five emperors already past, thus he is not now a threat, yet he will rise again to torment us. Swete reminds us that both Christian and pagan writers likened Domitian to his predecessor Nero.

The "ten horns" on the beast's seven heads represent "ten kings, who have received no kingdom as yet; but they receive authority as kings, with the beast, for one hour. These have one mind, and they give their power and authority unto the beast" (17:12-13). Conquered kings and rulers of countries allied with Rome – all of whom depended on Rome's favor for their right to retain power – have participated in her fornications in an effort to keep their position. They support Rome and will be allied with her in the final showdown between the Lamb and his enemies (i.e., the Battle of Armageddon). As surely as they have shared in the harlot's fornications, they will also share in her fate. "These shall war against the Lamb, and the Lamb shall overcome them, for he is Lord of lords, and King of kings" (17:14a).

At verse sixteen, Rome's fate at the hands of her former allies is predicted. When the tide of history turned against the once-powerful harlot, there would be a "falling out among thieves." As the angel explained it to John: "And the ten horns which thou sawest, and the beast, these shall hate the harlot, and shall make her desolate and naked, and shall eat her flesh, and shall burn her utterly with fire. For God did put in their hearts to do his mind, and to come to one mind, and to give their kingdom unto the beast, until the words of God should be accomplished" (17:16-17). This reveals how Rome's judgment in history would be accomplished; it was to be at the hands of other nations. God's providence overrules all human affairs to the accomplishment of his purposes.

The Doom of Babylon the Great

"After these things I saw another angel coming down out of heaven, having great authority; and the earth was lightened with his glory. And he cried with a mighty voice, saying, Fallen, fallen is Babylon the great, and is become a habitation of demons, and a hold of every unclean spirit, and a hold of every unclean and hateful bird. For by the wine of the wrath of her fornication all the nations are fallen; and the kings of the earth committed fornication with her, and the merchants of the earth waxed rich by the power of her wantonness" (18:1-3).

At the time John was seeing these things and writing the Revelation, Babylon had not fallen. Yet her overthrow was so certain that the angel spoke of it as an accomplished fact. Speaking prophetically, he looked into the future and saw the destruction of Rome as already finished. The reason for her overthrow is no secet to anyone.

At this point, a warning is sounded for the people of God to separate themselves completely from Babylon (18:4-8). The appeal is that the saints should "come out" and "have no fellowship with her sins." The appended warning is to the effect that all who share in her sins will have to share in the plagues coming upon her.

Do you ever get discouraged? Do you sometimes think the odds are so stacked against you that it is pointless to resist? Have you ever had the feeling that the harder you try to do right the harder it is to keep your head up and keep going at all? It seems easier to go ahead and give in just this once; let the wrong have its way this time, and thereby avoid another difficulty! It was going to seem that way to some of the Christians reading the book of Revelation at the close of the first century and for a couple of centuries following. Rome simply looked invincible to them, and resistance must have seemed so futile at times. The Christians needed to be encouraged to hold on and to look to the ultimate outcome of the struggle.

Lest anyone think that the fall of Rome would generate only praise to the Lord and no mourning for that great city and its empire, several verses picture the kings of earth in grief (vs. 9-20). They "weep and wail" over the harlot's fate and cry, "Woe, woe, the great city, Babylon, the strong city! for in one hour is thy judgment come." Not only these kings but merchants, shipmasters, and sailors are pictured as being distraught over the event.

But *why* are these people sad? There is no grief for Rome; it is purely selfish on their part. The kings of earth lament only that their partner in fornication is gone, thus depriving them of pleasure (18:9-10); the merchants grieve only because they no longer have the customers they once had (18:11-17a); and the shipmasters and sailors are in agony only because the collapse of the economy built upon Rome's extravagance leaves them without work and wages (18:17b-19). Sinners have few friends when pleasure turns to pain.

The reaction of the righteous to the fall of Rome is quite different: "Rejoice over her, thou heaven, and ye saints, and ye apostles, and ye prophets; for God hath judged your judgment on her" (18:20). Neither God nor his faithful people take any pleasure in the destruction of the wicked (Ezek. 33:11). But those who deliberately refuse his gracious salvation must pay a high price. The execution of divine wrath against such persons – especially if their sins have been hindering the work of the church – is a just act and elicits a justifiable reaction of praise from the saints.

Reminiscent of Jeremiah's symbolic act in Jeremiah 51:63-64, the angel who has been showing all these things to John portrayed the fall of Rome with a dramatic gesture. "And a strong angel took up a stone as it were a great millstone and cast it into the sea, saying, Thus with a mighty fall shall Babylon, the great city, be cast down, and shall be found no more at all. And the voice of harpers and minstrels and flute-players and trumpeters shall be heard no more at all in thee; and no craftsman, of whatsoever craft, shall be found any more at all in thee; and the voice of a mill shall be heard no more at all in thee; and the light of a lamp shall shine no more at all in thee; and the voice of the bridegroom and of the bride shall be heard no more at all in thee" (18:21-23a).

There would be no more "life as usual" in Rome after the wrath of God was visited upon her. The harlot would be destroyed, and all the business life, revelry, and normal social intercourse of her chief city would be interrupted. She was going to reap the fruits of her sins against the church (18:23-24).

Heaven's Response to Babylon's Fall

Rome has been destroyed! The empire has fallen, and its capital city is in ruins! With Babylon justly judged and overthrown, there is a mighty chorus of thanksgiving and praise to God in heaven. "A great voice of a great multitude in heaven" was heard by John. Its song was this: "Hallelujah; Salvation, and glory, and power, belong to our God: for true and righteous are his judgments; for he hath judged the great harlot, her that corrupted the earth with her fornication, and he hath avenged the blood of his servants at her hand" (19:1-2). Salvation, glory, and power were claimed by Rome. They never belonged to her. They belong to God alone.

The destruction of Rome leaves only a smoking ruin for John to see – like the destruction of ancient Sodom and Gomorrah (19:3). It is God alone now who is worshipped in the Apocalypse. The elders, living creatures, and all his servants ascribe him the praise he is due for the deliverance of his church and for the destruction of its enemy (19:4-5).

God had been in control all along, but many had lost sight of this truth due to the persecutions which had raged. He had never abdicated his throne to Rome. With that wicked empire overthrown, his reign in human history is obvious for all to see again. Thus we hear: "Hallelujah: for the Lord our God, the Almighty, reigneth" (19:6b).

What is in many ways the climactic scene of the entire Apocalypse is now at hand: The Lamb's bride has "made herself ready" by her faithfulness, and the time has come for the "marriage of the Lamb" (19:7).

This figure is rooted in the Old Testament imagery of God and Israel (cf. Hos. 2:19; Ezek. 16:7). Just as Yahweh was the bridegroom and Israel his beloved bride, so in the New Testament is the new Israel presented as the bride of Christ (Eph. 5:22-23). It is a beautiful imagery, for it leads us to think of the closest and most loving of all ties. Just as the love of a man and woman for each other in marriage is the most intimate and tender of all relationships, so is the relationship between Christ and his church tender, loving, and stronger than any power that might try to sever them.

The beautiful wedding gown of the bride of Christ contrasts dramatically with the gaudy display of the great harlot (cf. Rev. 17:4; 18:16). Her clothing is not showy or suggestive; it is pure and worthy of her bridegroom. "And it was given unto her that she should array herself in fine linen, bright and pure: for the fine linen is the righteous acts of the saints" (19:8).

The faithful of all the ages are bidden to share in the "marriage supper of the Lamb" (19:9) and to celebrate this great day. John's awe at such a triumphant and happy scene – after all the terrors witnessed earlier – caused him to bow before the angel revealing these things to him; he "fell down before his feet to worship him" (19:10). But there is no rank among servants of the Lord. Special offices, peculiar talents, and notable deeds may occur among us. Yet none is better than the other, and none receives the worship of his fellow servants. So the angel interrupted John's intention and said, "See thou do it not: I am a fellow-servant with thee and with thy brethren that hold the testimony of Jesus: worship God: for the testimony of Jesus is the spirit of prophecy" (19:10).

The Fate of the Dragon, Beast, and False Prophet

Turning for a moment from the scene of the marriage feast, the curtain of heaven is pulled aside once again to reveal Jesus as the Triumphant Christ in all his splendor. Riding a white horse (19:11) and with crowns upon his head (19:12), he rides forth in a victory procession.

"And he is arrayed in a garment sprinkled with blood: and his name is called the Word of God" (19:13). The blood on his garment is not that of martyrs but his own. This is the blood with which he has overcome and by which he has provided victory to the saints. No Christian of any generation defeats Satan in his own power. There is only one power great enough to conquer sin and the devil, and that power is the blood of Jesus. There is where faith focuses. There is where hope is generated. There is where triumph originates.

The victory which Christ has won for his saints allows them to follow him in purity (19:14). No enemy can stand before him and his advancing host, for a "sharp sword" proceeds from his mouth (19:15a); it is he who will tread the "winepress of the fierceness of the wrath of God, the Almighty" (19:15b).

The victory Christ has won and gives to his people proves that he alone has the right to rule over humankind. He alone is "KING OF KINGS AND LORD OF LORDS" (19:16).

In anticipation of the destruction of the dragon, beast, and false prophet – along with all who follow them – by the advancing Christ and his host, an angel comes on the scene to call all the vultures that fly in the sky to come and feed on the corpses of the defeated enemies of Christ and the church (19:17-18). This is called the "great supper of God" and contrasts with the joyous marriage supper of the Lamb. The tables have been turned in history. The time has come for the people of God to rejoice and for the persecutors of the church to reap as they have sown.

The dragon, beast, and false prophet called their forces together for a final, last-ditch stand against the Lamb and his forces in Revelation 16:13-16. [Note: Remember that we are now seeing details of the action that was earlier represented as the pouring out of the seven bowls of divine wrath. This is not a separate battle from the Battle of Armageddon; it is the detailed account of how that battle proceeded and wound up.] There was hardly a "battle" at all. The power of Christ is so all-encompassing that there was never a prospect of the dragon, beast, and false prophet waging even a successful holding action – much less a victorious campaign–against his advancing power.

"And I saw the beast, and the kings of the earth, and their armies, gathered together to make war against him that sat upon the horse, and against his army. And the beast was taken, and with him the false prophet that wrought the signs in his sight, wherewith he deceived them that had received the mark of the beast and them that worshipped his image: they two were cast alive into the lake of fire that burneth with brimstone: and the rest were killed with the sword of him that sat upon the horse, even the sword which came forth out of his mouth: and all the birds were filled with their flesh" (19:19-21).

Rome is seen in ruins. With her fall in 476 A.D., Satan's great allies in persecuting the church were destroyed. The beast (i.e., the Roman emperors) and the false prophet (i.e., the cult of emperor worship) were thrown into the lake that burns with fire and brimstone. Now there is only one enemy left to be dealt with, and that is the dragon himself (i.e., Satan).

The one who has been behind all the troubles of the church has not escaped. He is simply being dealt with last.

An angel of God descended from heaven with a "great chain" in his hand (20:1). He took hold of the old dragon and "bound him for a thousand years" (20:2). The figure 1,000 has been used numbers of times in Revelation to signify completeness. Binding Satan for a thousand years indicates that Satan has been stripped of the terrible powers he exercised during Rome's persecution of the church for the duration of the Christian Age. He will never have such power again during the time between Rome's fall and the second coming of Christ.

Notice that Satan is "bound" but not destroyed (20:3). As Rome fell, Satan was bound insofar as his powers to "deceive the nations" are concerned. Earlier in the Apocalypse we learned that the dragon had been allowed to empower the beast "to make war with the saints, and to overcome them: and there was given to him authority over every tribe and people and tongue and nation" (Rev. 13:7). That power was stripped from him when Rome fell.

The loosing of Satan at the end of the thousand years is much more difficult to interpret than the meaning of the millennium itself. Will he begin to create a world power on the order of Rome (i.e., one hostile to the church) in the last days of the world (cf. 20:7-8)? Or is his release at that time merely a prelude to calling him into final Judgment and casting him into the lake of fire and brimstone for his destruction along with his allies? In view of the fact that Jesus said there would be no special sign of the end of the world and his second coming (Matt. 24:36-44), the latter interpretation would appear more reasonable.

In connection with the binding of Satan for a thousand years, those "souls beheaded for the testimony of Jesus" under Rome's time of persecution are allowed to reign with their Lord. This reign is in heaven rather than on earth (i.e., where the "thrones" of Revelation are located); it is a reign shared with the martyrs of Rome's persecution, not all saints; it is not connected with the second coming but with the fall of Rome. These points are usually overlooked by those who want to find an earthly reign of Christ in these verses.

As a matter of fact, the notion of a thousand-year reign of Christ on earth from David's throne in Jerusalem is unbiblical. In connection with the fall of Judah and the taking of the last king of the Davidic dynasty into captivity in 606 B.C., it was prophesied that no one among his descendants would succeed in reigning from David's throne in Jerusalem ever again (Jer. 22:30). Interestingly enough, that very king (i.e., Jeconiah) is in the lineage of Jesus of Nazareth (Matt. 1:11-12), thus disqualifying him from the sort of earthly reign which so many envision for him. Christ's reign with his faithful martyrs from heaven is the millennium of Revelation 20, not some future reign on planet earth for a period of peace and utopian contentment.

The exaltation of the martyrs to vindication and glory is called the "first resurrection" (20:5). There will be one and only one *bodily* resurrection of the dead, and that will occur for all people at Jesus' second coming in glory (cf. John 5:28-29). Thus the first resurrection is a way of referring to the triumph of the martyrs in connection with the fall of Rome, and the "second resurrection" – never mentioned but implied here – must be the general resurrection of the dead at Christ's return. Those vindicated in that first resurrection need have no fear of the "second death" (i.e., the lake of fire and brimstone into which the beast and false prophet have been cast already, 20:6; cf. 20:14).

At the end of the thousand-year reign of the martyrs with Christ, Satan will be "loosed" from the abyss (20:7), he will assemble the hosts of wickedness for one last time under "Gog and Magog" (20:8), and will make a final attempt to destroy the church (20:9a). This is not the Battle of Armageddon, for in our drama it was fought at the start of the thousand-year reign; this battle comes at the end. This is the final gathering of all the wicked for Judgment before the Lord. In Jewish apocalyptic literature, Gog and Magog often symbolize the forces of evil; here they are seen assembled for one last time. But whatever hope they have of triumphing over the Lamb in connection with such an assembly is dashed immediately. "Fire came down out of heaven, and devoured them" (20:9b).

In this final confrontation, Satan himself is dealt with once and for all. He is sent to share the fate of the beast and false prophet. "And the devil that deceived them was cast into the lake of fire and brimstone, where are also the beast and the false prophet; and they shall be tormented day and night for ever and ever" (20:10).

Conclusion

The drama of the Apocalypse is finished! The conflict between the Lamb and his enemies has been concluded, and *the Lamb has conquered!*

The message of hope, comfort, and encouragement to the first-century Christians who originally received this book is clear. Be faithful to the Lamb, for the victory belongs to him. No power can stand before the Almighty God. If you would share in his triumph, stand with him in your moment of trial!

For the Christian of any age, the message is essentially the same. Do you have a mighty foe? Is there some ordeal or persecution you must face? No obstacle is greater than the power of the Lamb. Put your trust in him, be faithful to him, and resist all efforts to compromise your integrity as his follower. The victory is assured, for the Lamb has conquered.

Thinking Through Chapter Twelve

1. Who is the "great harlot" of Revelation? Contrast her with the bride of Christ.

2. What relationship does the harlot have with the scarlet-colored beast? Have we met this character before in our drama? Identify the beast.

3. A name was written on the harlot's forehead. Discuss its significance.

4. What is the cryptic meaning of verse eleven?

5. What was to be the fate of Rome at the hands of her former allies?

6. Why was Rome destined to suffer such a horrible fate?

7. Describe the reaction of heaven to the fall of Rome.

8. How do the dragon, beast, and false prophet band together for one final time? How does this battle relate to the Battle of Armageddon?

9. What is the thousand-year period anticipated in this context? What was Satan's fate during it? What of the Lamb and his followers?

10. What is the "first resurrection"? What is the "second resurrection"?

Chapter Thirteen

The Eternal Destiny of the Redeemed
Revelation 20:11-22:21

The bulk of the book of Revelation has to do with the judgments of God within history, particularly his judgments against wicked Rome for her persecution of the church. Beginning with chapter four, these judgments have been portrayed in apocalyptic symbols. The message of the book would have been complete if the Apocalypse had ended with Revelation 20:10.

But the Holy Spirit did not conclude the book with the overthrow of Rome and her allies. He allowed John to leap forward from that time in history to the consummation of all things at the return of Jesus. At Revelation 20:11 we move far beyond the time of divine judgments within history to the final Judgment of the entire world.

The scene of Judgment here is fully consistent with every other fact revealed about that day in the remainder of the New Testament. All humanity will be gathered before the great throne of the Lord, judgment will be rendered according to the deeds done in the flesh, and the decision rendered to each person will be final and irrevocable.

In this section of the Apocalypse, we see the complete drama of human redemption brought to its final act.

The Final Judgment

The scene before the great white throne is an awe-inspiring one. "And I saw a great white throne, and him that sat upon it, from whose face the earth and the heaven fled away; and there was found no place for them. And I saw the dead, the great and the small, standing before the throne; and books were opened: and another book was opened, which is the book of life: and the dead were judged out of the things which were written in the books, according to their works" (20:11-12).

Throughout the Apocalypse it has been God the Father who is seen seated on the throne in heaven. Yet God the Son is presented as the judge of all men on the last great day in passages such as Acts 17:31. Is there some conflict or contradiction in Scripture on this point? There is no problem, for John has already made the matter clear in the information he gave in his Gospel. He quoted Jesus as having said: "For neither doth the Father judge any man, but he hath given all judgment unto the Son; that all may honor the Son, even as they honor the Father" (John 5:22-23a). The actions of Father, Son, and Holy Spirit are always those of one God. When the Bible affirms that God is "one" (cf. Deut. 6:4), such statements are not to be understood in terms of the numerical digit (i.e., "1" in the number sequence 0, 1, 2, 3, etc.) but as references to the divine unity (e.g., Gen. 2:24; John 17:22; Gal. 3:28) which pervades all the works of God.

With this hour of final Judgment upon humanity having come, heaven and earth are pictured as fleeing away. This is further explained when John adds the comment that there was "no place for them." This seems to indicate that the cosmos we know through our physical senses simply ceased to exist in John's vision; they were destroyed utterly and finally. This certainly fits with what we know of the second coming of Christ through Peter's writings. After saying that his return would catch many off guard and unprepared, he wrote: "The heavens shall pass away with a great noise, and the elements shall be dissolved with fervent heat, and the earth and the works that are therein shall be burned up" (2 Pet. 3:10b).

With the physical heavens and earth gone, the focus of attention is centered exclusively on the throne, its occupant, and all those assembled before it. All people from the various millennia of earth's history – "the great and the small" – were seen before the throne. The signal that their judgment was about to begin was given in the opening of the "books" by him who sat upon the throne. John does not identify these books. Some have suggested that they represent the various covenants under which men have lived at different times in history. In view of the fact that judgment will be based on "their works," it seems more likely that the books contain the records of the deeds of men's lives on earth.

Then another book is opened which is identified for us. It is "the book of life." It is the citizenship roll of the New Jerusalem (cf. Ex. 32:32; Mal. 3:16; Luke 10:20; Phil. 4:3; Rev. 3:5). This book contains the names of God's elect, called, and chosen people. Those whose names are written in the book of life have nothing to fear in standing before the throne. Those whose names are not found there stand before the throne without hope, for "if any was not found written in the book of life, he was cast into the lake of fire" (20:15).

That this judgment will proceed "according to their works" (20:13) should not be misunderstood. The Bible teaches that salvation is by grace through faith (Eph. 2:8-9). That no person can be saved by his own good deeds is taught everywhere in both Old and New Testaments. John is not departing from that theme here. To say that judgment will be based on "works" in this context is simply to say that it will take into account all the deeds of one's life on earth. Surely the principal work of each individual which is entered into those record books is the account of his or her response to Christ and his offer of pardon through his blood.

While living in the flesh on planet earth, each of us makes a response to Jesus Christ. We respond either in faith or in unbelief. We either commit to his Lordship and live to his glory, or we resist him and continue to walk in our own impenitent ways. It is that response which is of first importance in the record books of the deeds of men. Other facts about sacrifices made or services rendered for the sake of Christ will be taken into account in determining the degree of one's reward (cf. 1 Cor. 3:10-15), but the fact of one's responsive and submissive faith in Jesus is the crucial matter. Other facts about blasphemies and deliberate oppositions to Jesus will be taken into account in fixing the degree of one's punishment (cf. Luke 12:47-48), but the determining factor which will separate him from the Lord eternally is his unbelief.

John also witnessed the fate of death and Hades in this scene. "And death and Hades were cast into the lake of fire. This is the second death, even the lake of fire" (20:14). Death is the common fate of mankind, and Hades is the common destination of humanity. After both have delivered up all that are in them, they are simply destroyed. They are done away with, for they have no further purpose to serve.

It is interesting to note, however, that John does not concentrate on the lake of fire and those things and persons cast into it. His chief concern is to describe the glories of the redeemed in the New Jerusalem.

The New Jerusalem

"Now that all evil has been destroyed for ever, and all evil agents have been cast into the lake of fire, that the former heaven and earth have vanished, the final judgment brought to a close, and death and Hades destroyed, God creates a new heaven and earth, and summons into being the New Jerusalem" (Charles).

When Peter anticipated the destruction of the physical heavens and earth in the passage cited earlier, he pointed forward to a new environment for the redeemed of God. He wrote: "But, according to his promise, we look for new heavens and a new earth, wherein dwelleth righteousness" (2 Pet. 3:13). In his vision of the summation of all things related to the redemption drama of the Apocalypse, John saw this divine promise being fulfilled (21:1).

In particular, his attention was riveted on the holy city which appeared to be the central focus of the new cosmos. "And I saw the holy city, new Jerusalem, coming down out of heaven from God, made ready as a bride adorned for her husband" (21:2). New Jerusalem is heaven as it has been prepared for the redeemed church (cf. Heb. 12:22). It is "as a bride adorned for her husband." Unlike the awful harlot seen earlier in the Revelation, she has kept herself pure from defilement and is prepared for her permanent union with Christ.

In this holy city, all distance between God and his people is removed. "And I heard a great voice out of the throne saying, Behold, the tabernacle of God is with men, and he shall dwell with them, and they shall be his peoples, and God himself shall be with them, and be their God" (21:3). Life on earth is a probationary experience for the creatures of

113

God. We have evidences of the existence and presence of deity in this life, but we nevertheless worship him from afar and are sometimes subjected to awful pressures – as were the saints who suffered under Rome – designed to draw us away from him. In heaven one is in the immediate presence of God, looks upon his very person, and worships him without distraction. No trials or temptations can enter heaven to interrupt this perfect fellowship.

In fact, life in heaven has no inadequacies or unsatisfied needs of any sort. Death, mourning, crying, pain, and the "first things" (i.e., things as they were known previously on earth) are done away with there (21:4-7). The tormented saints of the first century were being told by John that their present state was not to be their final one. Suffering Christians of our own time may take heart on the basis of the same certainty.

Those who are not part of the redeemed church at the return of Christ have a very different and horrible fate awaiting them. They will have to share in the same "second death" to which the dragon, beast, and false prophet have already been condemned (21:8).

John gives a rather detailed description of the holy city he saw. One of the seven angels he had seen earlier in connection with the overthrow of Rome carried him "in the Spirit" to a high mountain; from this vantage point, he was allowed to survey the city with deliberate care (21:9-10).

God's own glory fills the place (21:11), and its absolute security is guaranteed by a "wall great and high" which surrounds it (21:12a). The twelve gates to the city have the names of the twelve tribes of Israel written on them (21:12b-13). This emphasizes the restriction placed upon entry into the city; it is the home of God and those people from off the earth who have been cleansed by the blood of the Lamb (cf. Rev. 7). On the twelve foundations of the holy city are written the names of the twelve apostles (21:14). This honor goes to the Twelve because of their faithful proclamation of the gospel and the establishment of the church through their labors (cf. Eph. 2:19-20).

This holy city is a perfect cube (21:15-21). Remembering the dimensions of the holy of holies in the temple (cf. 1 Kings 6:20), surely John is telling his readers that this is the ultimate holy place. The inner precinct has been entered by all the priests of God, and the glory of the Almighty overshadows all else. This is why there is no temple external to God's own presence in the city. "And I saw no temple therein: for the Lord God the Almighty, and the Lamb, are the temple thereof" (21:22). The twelve precious stones mentioned in this context (21:19b-20) are thought by some scholars to be equivalent to the twelve stones in the high priest's breastplate (cf. Ex. 28:17-20). If so, verses fifteen through twenty form an extended parallel between the earthly temple that was so important to Old Testament Israel and the heavenly temple which means everything to New Testament Israel.

Whereas some interpretations of the Apocalypse anticipate an earthly paradise with a rebuilt (physical) temple in (physical) Jerusalem as the goal of the drama of this book, this passage about the location and nature of the temple of God seems to destroy such theories altogether.

The glory of New Jerusalem is so overwhelming that all other glories fade into it and become meaningless by comparison. "And the nations shall walk amidst the light thereof: and the kings of the earth bring their glory into it. And the gates thereof shall in no wise be shut by day (for there shall be no night there): and they shall bring the glory and the honor of the nations into it" (21:24-26).

In the midst of his description of heaven, John surely feels the limitations of human language for such a task. How does one put the glories of the New Jerusalem into words? For the lack of a better way to proceed, he simply resorts to a few negative descriptive terms. "And there shall in no wise enter into it anything unclean, or he that maketh an abomination and a lie. ... And there shall be no curse any more" (21:27a; 22:3a). The things that have been hateful and damaging to the church on earth cannot enter her final abode to inflict more pain or harm.

"And he showed me a river of water of life, bright as crystal, proceeding out of the throne of God and of the Lamb, in the midst of the street thereof. And on this side of the river and on that was the tree of life, bearing twelve manner of fruits, yielding its fruit every month: and the leaves of the tree were for the healing of the nations" (22:1-2). Summers points out that these verses identify the three basic things necessary to life (i.e., water, food, and health) and portray the ability of God to meet these needs for his people. "The water of life and the perpetual fruit of the tree of life furnish the food and drink; the leaves with their healing powers furnish health. Together they symbolize God's nurture and care for his own. How can a man live forever? Here is the answer, and it comes from 'the throne of God and of the Lamb' – God has all that is needed to sustain eternal life in man."

Here the very face of God will be seen by those with him (22:4; cf. Ex. 33:20; John 1:18), and the redeemed will share in the eternal reign of the God whose love and grace have saved them (22:5).

Wrapping Up the Apocalypse

The story is finished. The drama is complete, and the curtain has been brought down. Revelation 22:6-21 constitutes an *epilogue* to the book and stresses the importance of what has been revealed in it. First, there is an authentication of its contents as being from God. Second, there is an assurance of the nearness of its fulfillment.

"And he said unto me, These words are faithful and true: and the Lord, the God of the spirits of the prophets, sent his angel to show unto his servants the things which must shortly come to pass. And behold, I come quickly. Blessed is he that keepeth the words of the prophecy of this book" (22:6-7).

These words surely came through the revealing angel who has been showing John the various things in this book (cf. 22:8b,16a). "These words are faithful and true" is a guarantee concerning the entire book of Revelation. The reminder that all these things "must shortly come to pass" stands as a warning against the kind of abuse to which the book has been put so often. Revelation is abused by those who try to find in it a blueprint for our time; it is a document to persecuted saints of the first century about the outcome of their trials. Its enduring lessons and principles are for all generations, but its specific prophecies about human history have already been fulfilled at our point in time. The "I come quickly" statement of verse seven has to do with the unfolding events against Rome (i.e., judgments in history) rather than the personal coming of Jesus in final Judgment.

Next John adds his attestation that this book was written by his own hand and contains visions and revelations given him by the Lord. "And I John am he that heard and saw these things. And when I heard and saw, I fell down to worship before the feet of the angel that showed me these things. And he saith unto me, See thou do it not: I am a fellow-servant with thee and with thy brethren the prophets, and with them that keep the words of this book: worship God" (22:8-9).

Finally, there is a warning for John's readers to heed the message of the Apocalypse. Speaking for Jesus himself, the angel tells John not to seal it away for future generations; the things in this book will come to pass soon (22:10-13). Thus mankind must be prepared in view of the Lord's searching judgments which are about to begin (22:14).

To give ultimate emphasis to the importance of this book and the urgency of heeding its message, Jesus himself speaks to authenticate its truthfulness. "I Jesus have sent mine angel to testify unto you these things for the churches. I am the root and the offspring of David, the bright, the morning star" (22:16).

The final call to repentance and salvation by means of which one can escape the awful fate of the wicked pictured in Revelation is given in these words: "And the Spirit and the bride say, Come. And he that heareth, let him say, Come. And he that is athirst, let him come: he that will, let him take the water of life freely" (22:17). The contents of the book will not be changed (22:18-19), thus one who reads or hears it must take it seriously and act quickly.

As Jesus said to John "Yea: I come quickly [to execute the judgments pictured in this book]," John surely thought of the horrible things happening to his brethren back on the mainland of Asia and responded, "Amen: come, Lord Jesus" (22:20). The Lord responded to this prayer and the others like it from beleaguered saints of the late first century and brought their oppressor down with a horrible devastation.

Conclusion

What joy the delivery of this book must have produced in the hearts of its original recipients! They could not foresee the outcome of their struggle, but the God who has all of history under his view – future as well as past or present – could foresee its end. Now he had revealed it to them. They were allowed to know that the victory was assured to the Lamb. Yes, the Lamb has enemies. But they cannot conquer him, for the kingdom, the power, and the glory belong to him alone.

"The grace of the Lord Jesus be with the saints. Amen" (22:21).

Thinking Through Chapter Thirteen

1. Who will be the judge at the last day? Is there a conflict between the Apocalypse and Acts 17:31 on this point?

2. Why are earth and heaven pictured as fleeing on Judgment Day?

3. What "books" will be used in connection with the Judgment?

4. What is meant when Scripture says judgment will be rendered to men "according to their works"?

5. Identify the shared fate of death and Hades.

6. Relate the prospect envisioned at 2 Peter 3:13 to the scene witnessed by John in the Revelation.

7. How will life in heaven compare with the life we know on earth?

8. What negative descriptive terms did John employ to describe heaven?

9. Discuss the various elements of the epilogue to Revelation.

10. What effect do you think this book would have had on the saints of the Roman province of Asia when they first received it? What is its abiding value for Christians of all ages?

Bibliography

The titles listed here are among the more helpful reference works which relate to the book of Revelation. They are referred to in the text of this volume by the author's last name. Unless specific page numbers are cited from them, any quotations from these books are from the section dealing with the passage under examination in this volume.

Barclay, William. *Letters to the Seven Churches*. Nashville: Abingdon Press, 1957.

Beasley-Murray, G. R. *The Book of Revelation*, rev. ed. *New Century Bible*. Edited by Ronald E. Clements and Matthew Black. Greenwood, SC: Attic Press, Inc., 1978.

Bettenson, Henry, ed. *Documents of the Christian Church*, 2nd ed. London: Oxford University Press, 1963.

Caird, G. B. *A Commentary on the Revelation of St. John the Divine. Harper's New Testament Commentaries*. Edited by Henry Chadwick. New York: Harper & Row, Publishers, 1966.

Charles, R. H. *A Critical and Exegetical Commentary on the Revelation of St. John*. 2 vols. *International Critical Commentary*. Edited by S. R. Driver, A. Plummer, and C. A. Briggs. Edinburgh: T. & T. Clark, 1920.

Guthrie, Donald. *New Testament Introduction*, 3rd ed. rev. Downers Grove, IL: Inter-Varsity Press, 1970.

Hendriksen, William. *More Than Conquerors: An Interpretation of the Book of Revelation*. Grand Rapids: Baker Book House, 1940.

Morris, Leon. *The Revelation of St. John. Tyndale New Testament Commentaries*. Edited by R. V. G. Tasker. Grand Rapids: William B. Eerdmans Publishing Company, 1969.

Mounce, Robert H. *The Book of Revelation. New International Commentary on the New Testament*. Edited by F. F. Bruce. Grand Rapids: William B. Eerdman's Publishing Company, 1977.

Roberts, J. W. *The Revelation to John. The Living Word Commentary*. Edited by Everett Ferguson. Austin, TX: Sweet Publishing Company, 1974.

Schmithals, Walter. *The Apocalyptic Movement: Introduction and Interpretation*. Trans. John E. Steely. Nashville: Abingdon Press, 1975.

Summers, Ray. *Worthy is the Lamb*. Nashville: Broadman Press, 1951.

Swete, Henry Barclay. *Commentary on Revelation*, 3rd ed. London: Macmillan Co., 1911. Reprinted; Grand Rapids: Kregel Publications, 1977.

CPSIA information can be obtained at www.ICGtesting.com
Printed in the USA
LVOW13s0448061113

360097LV00002B/2/P